I0442583

This Journal Belongs To:

Without your voice we don't exist.

Please, support us and leave a review

★ ★ ★ ★ ★

Thank you!

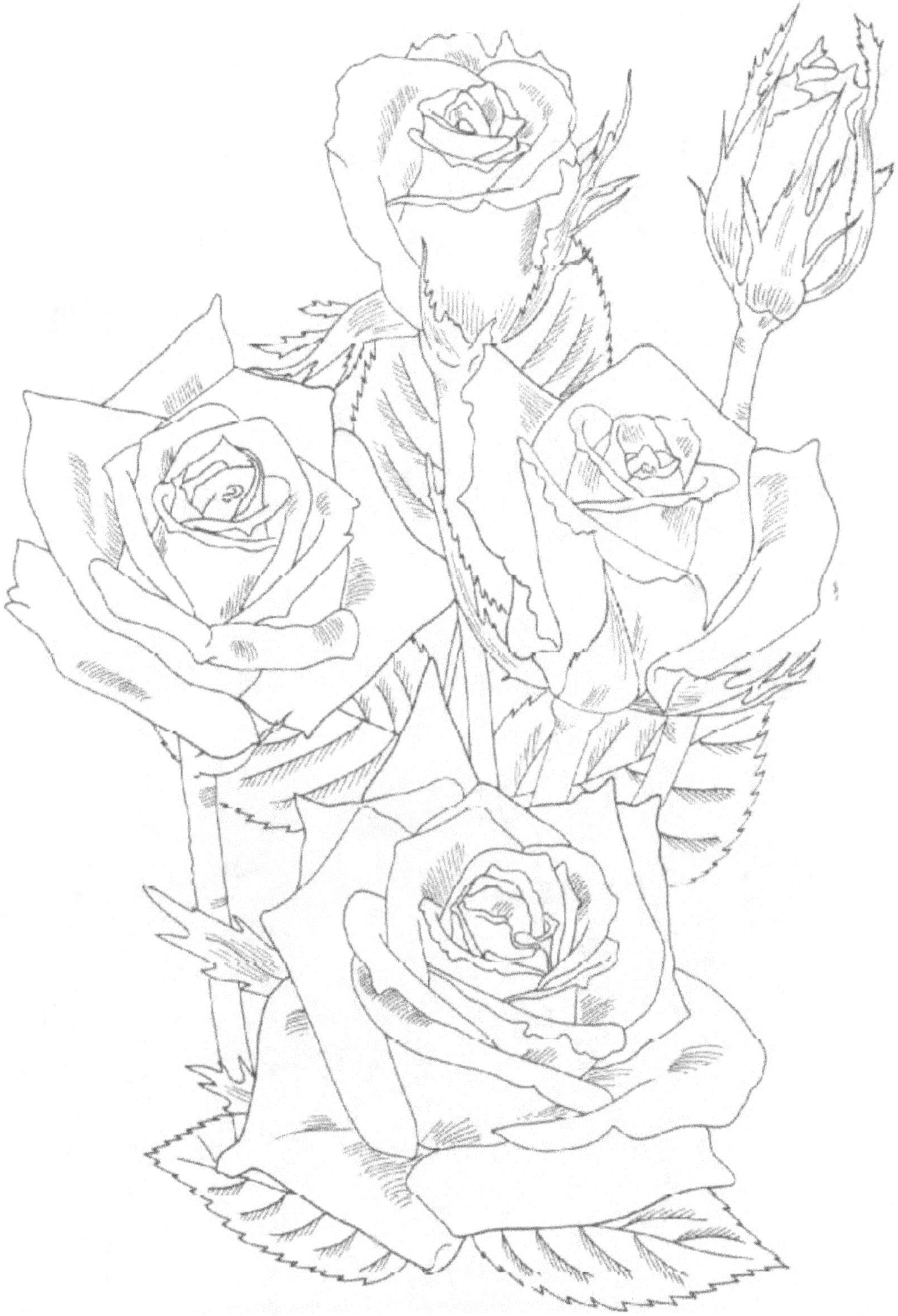

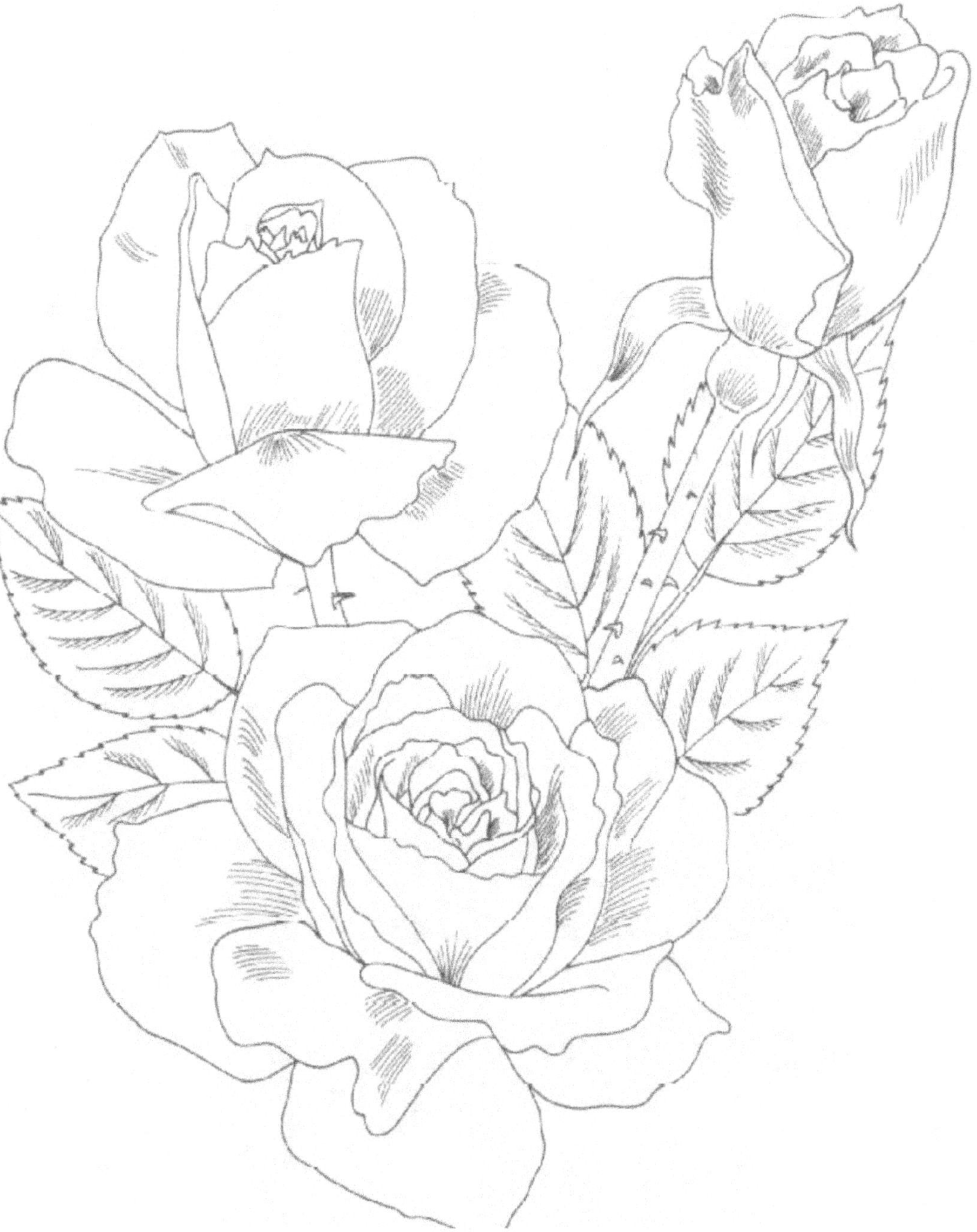

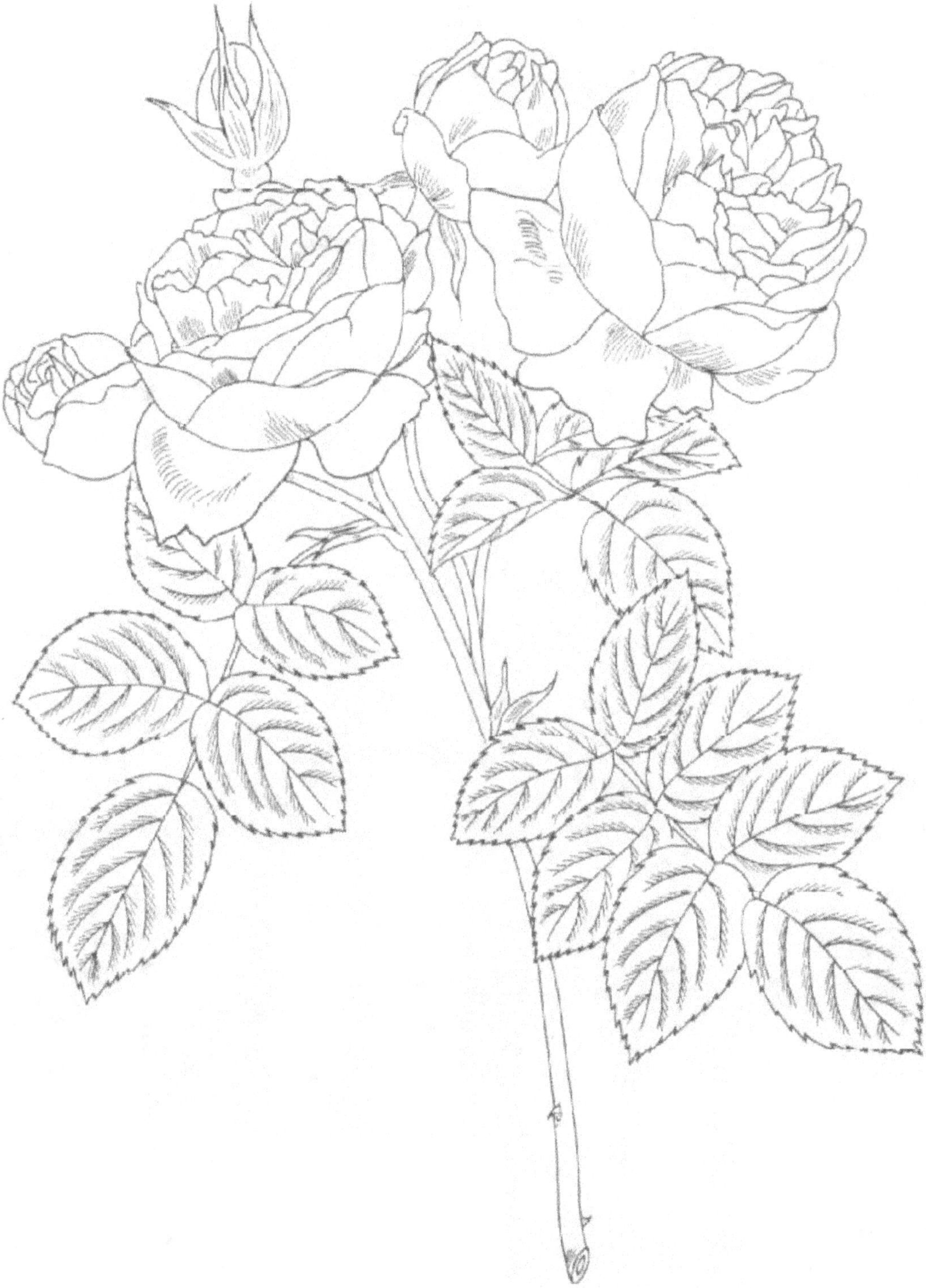

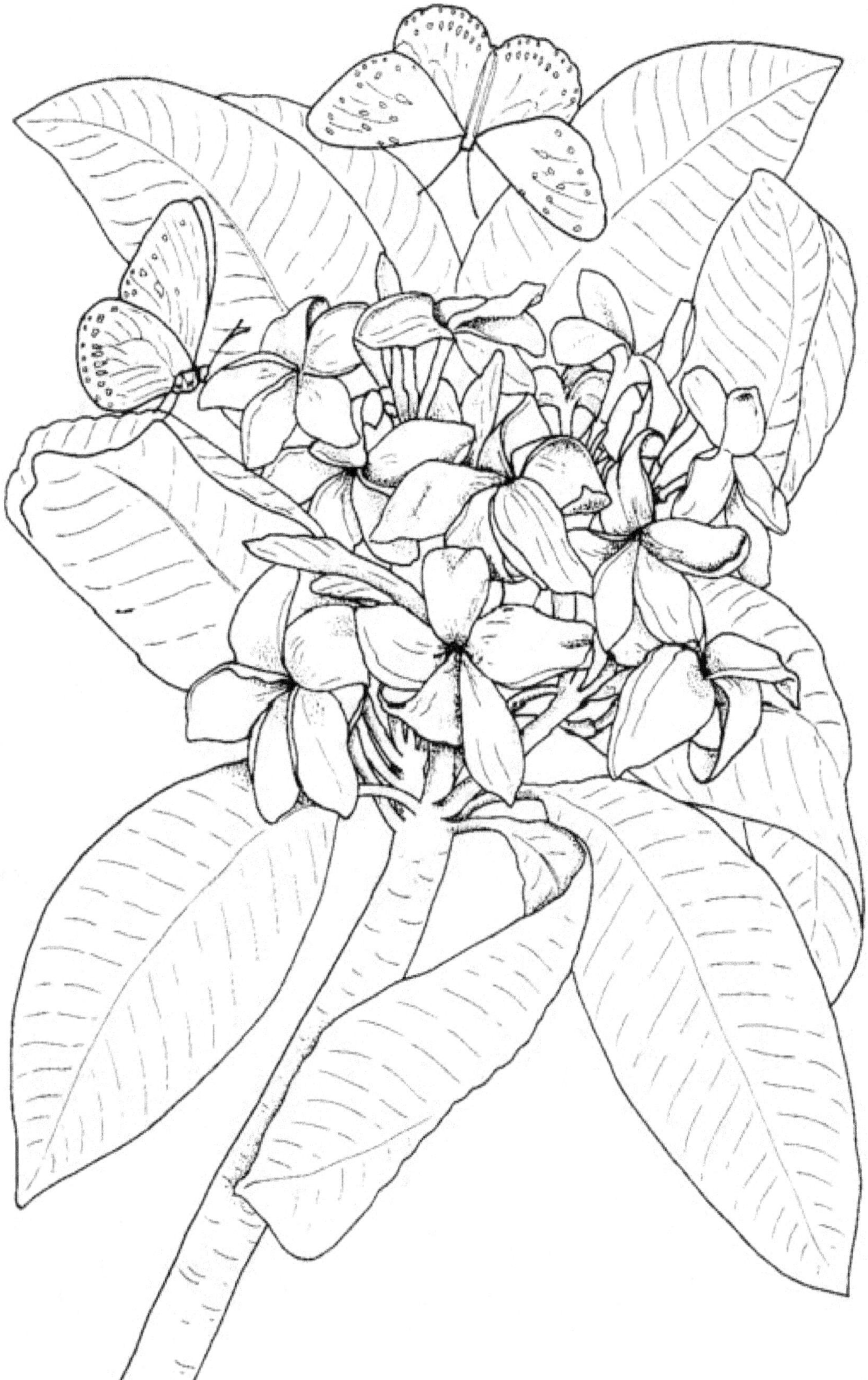

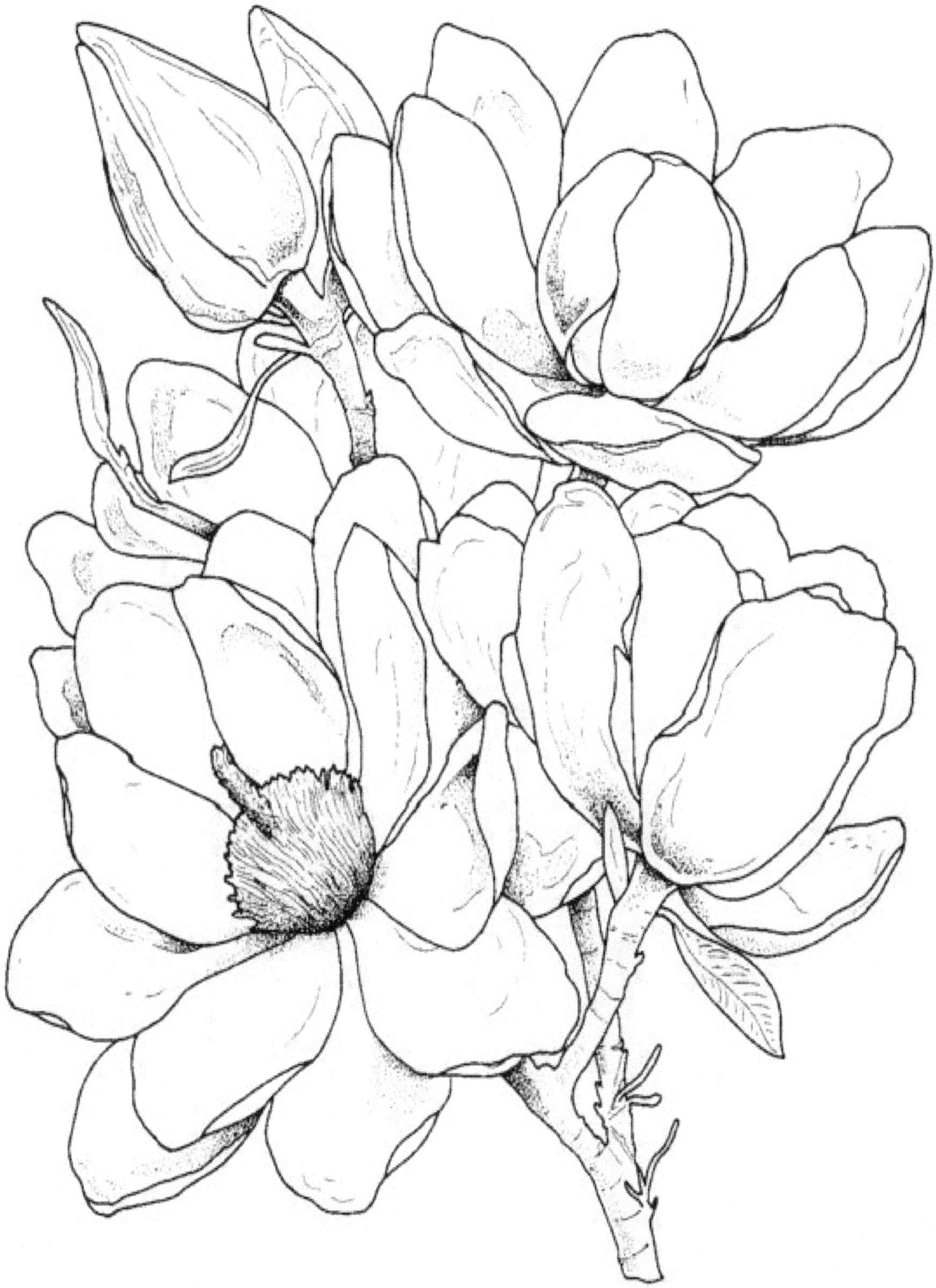

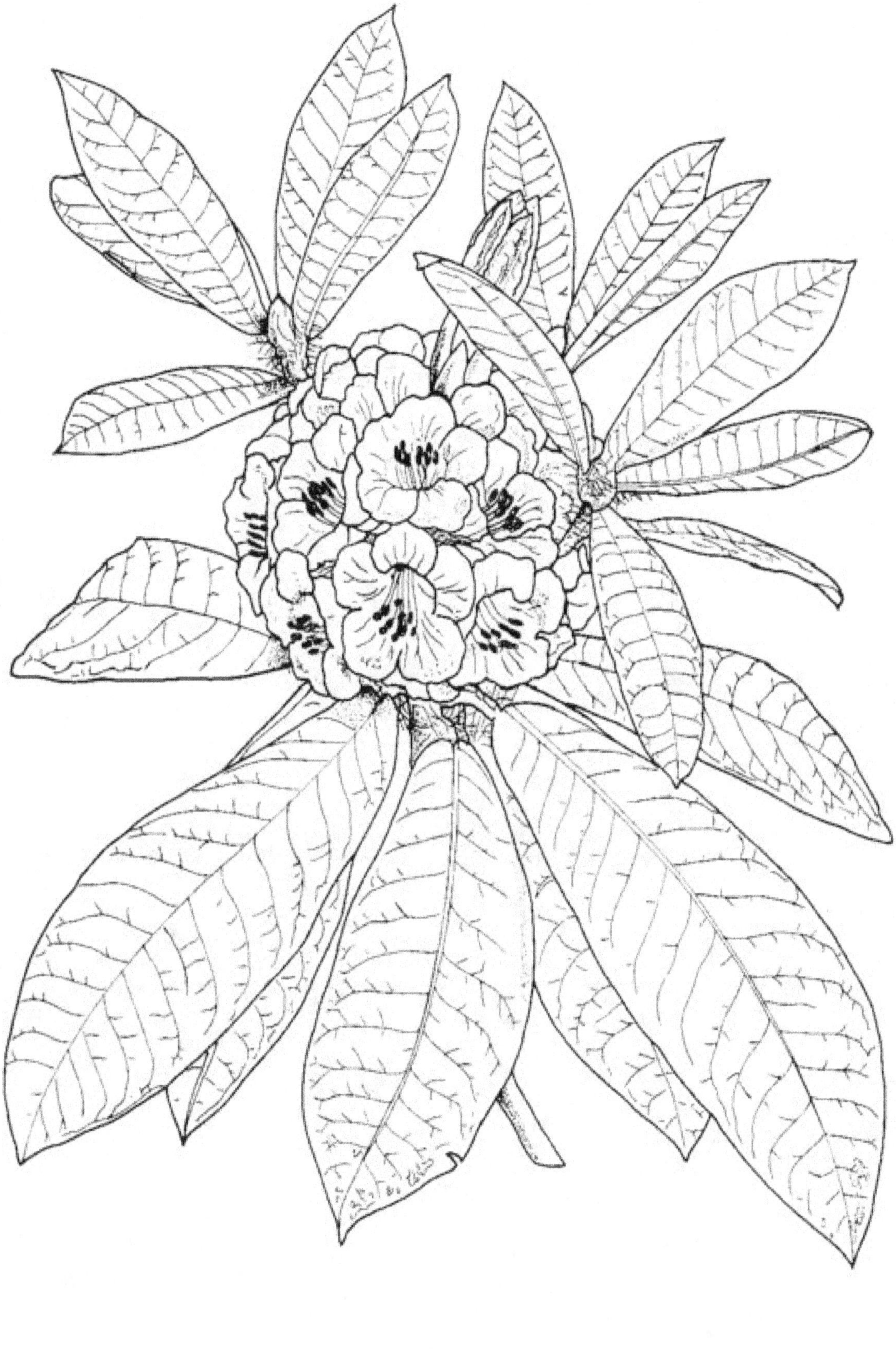

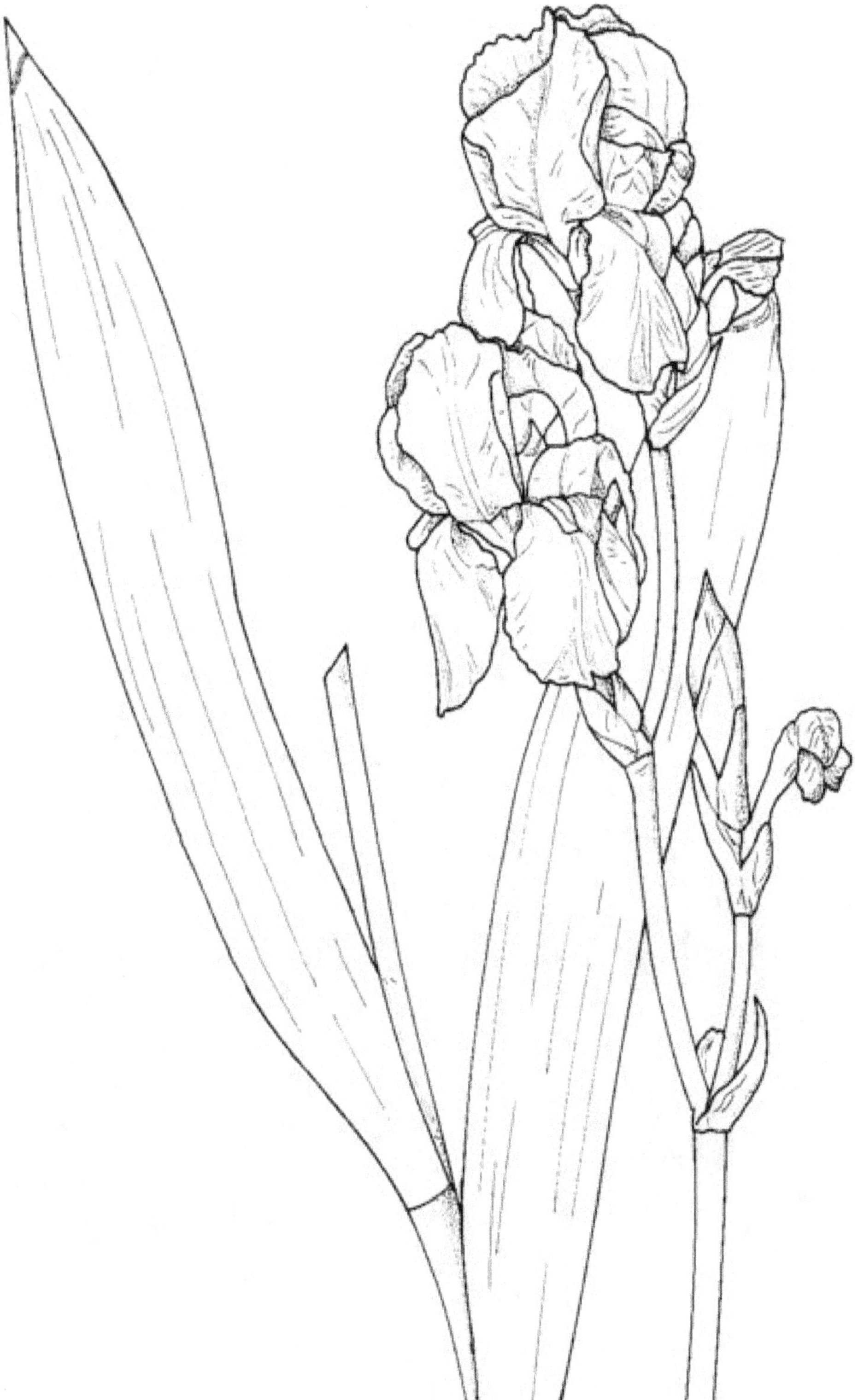

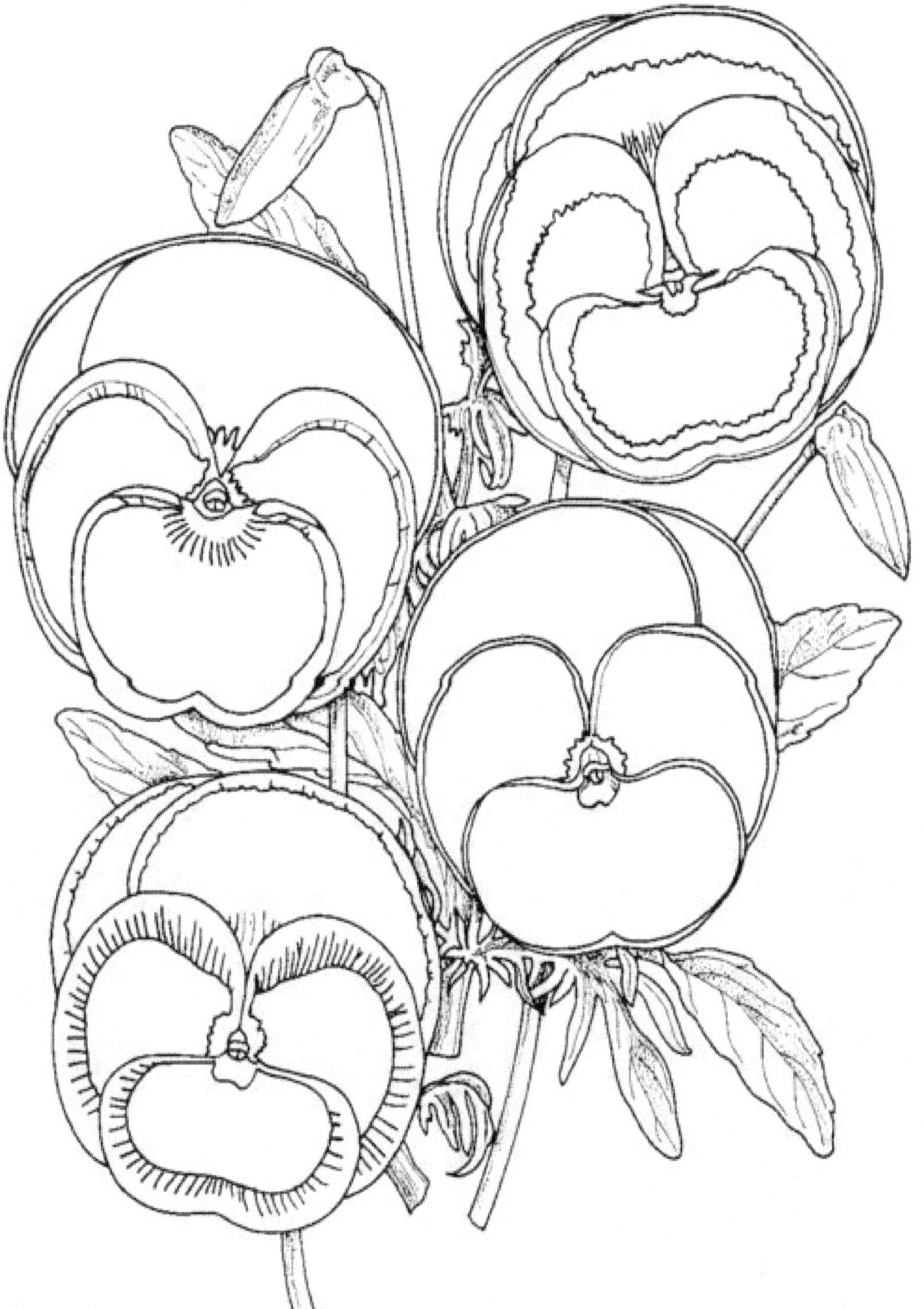

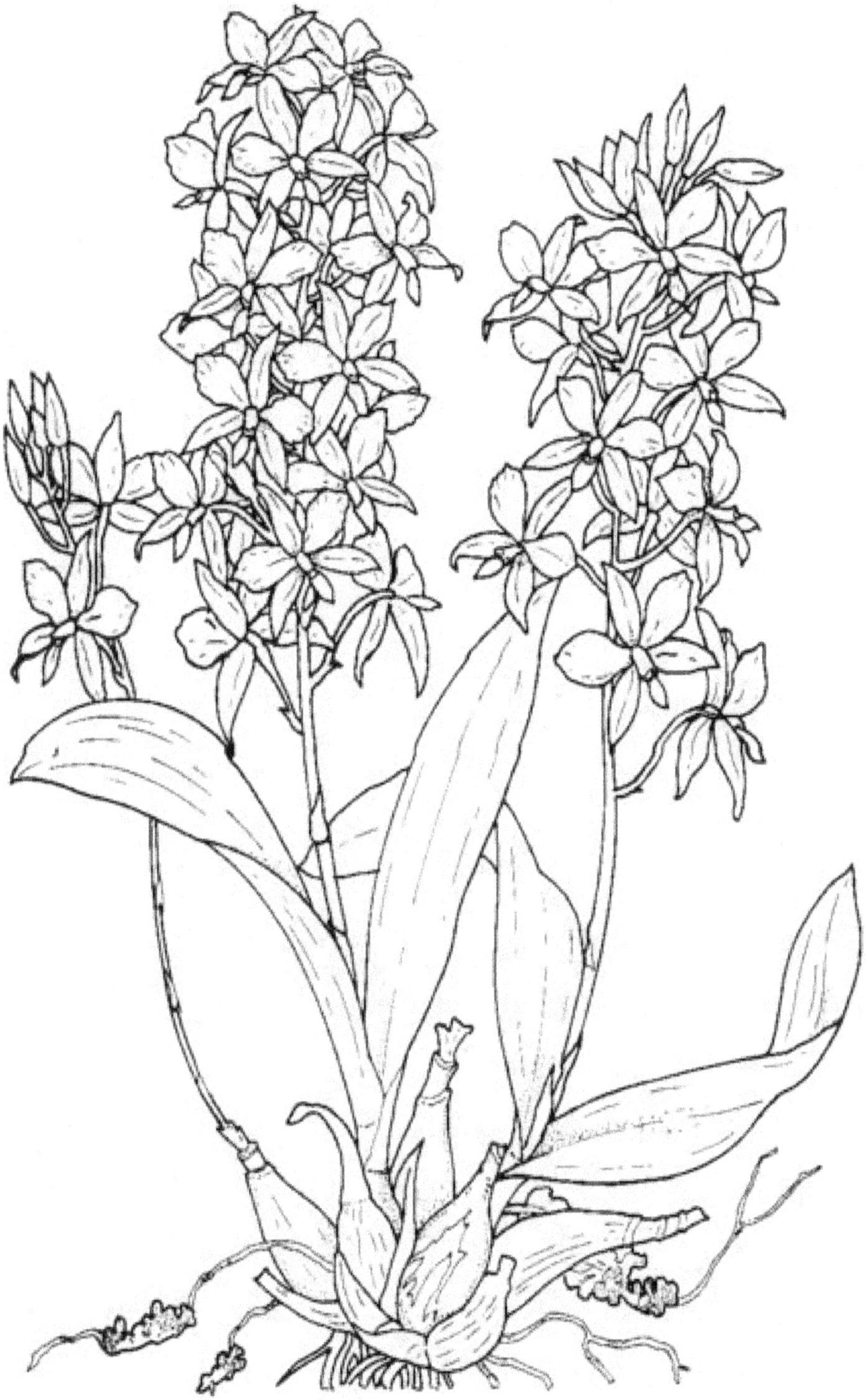

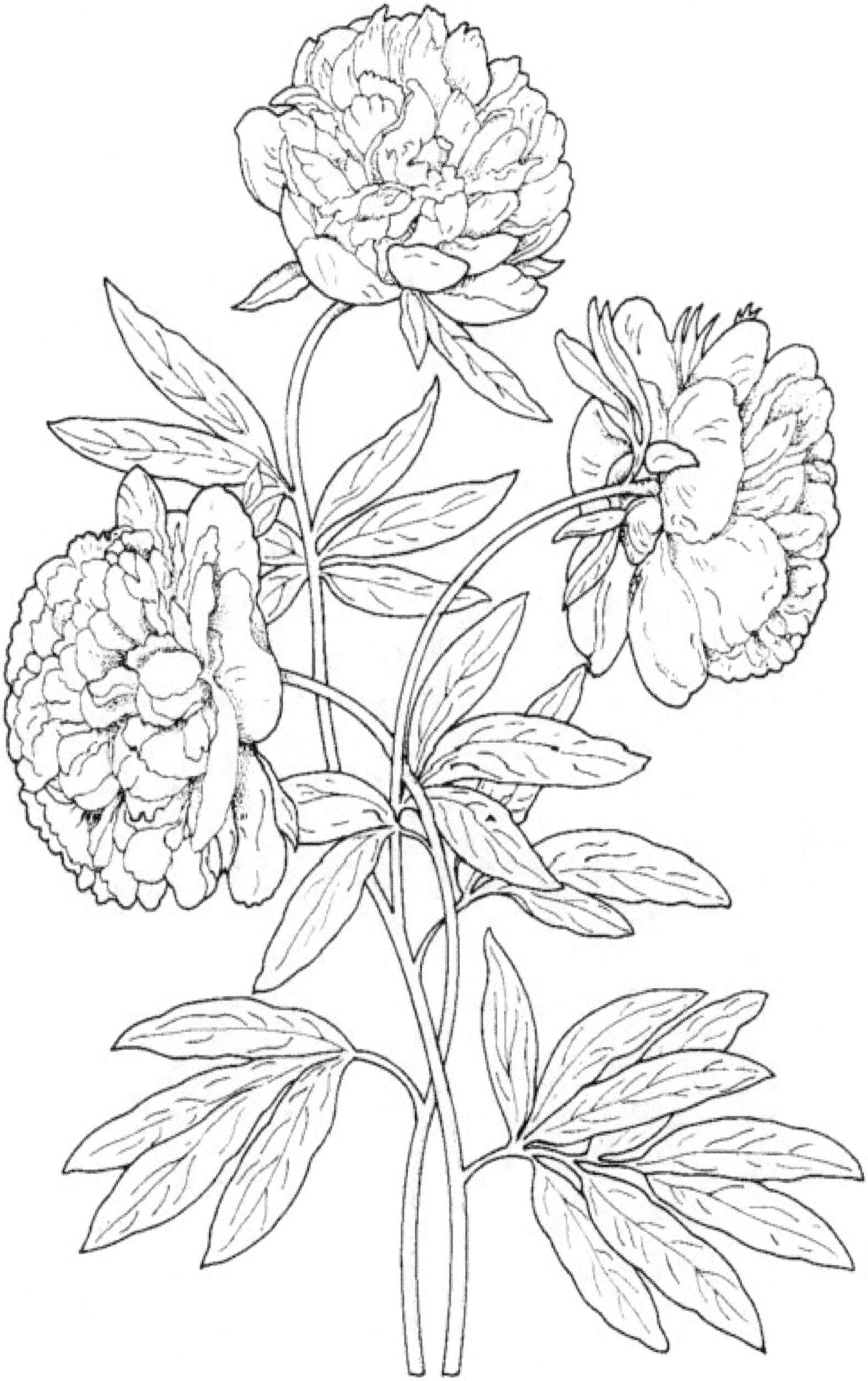

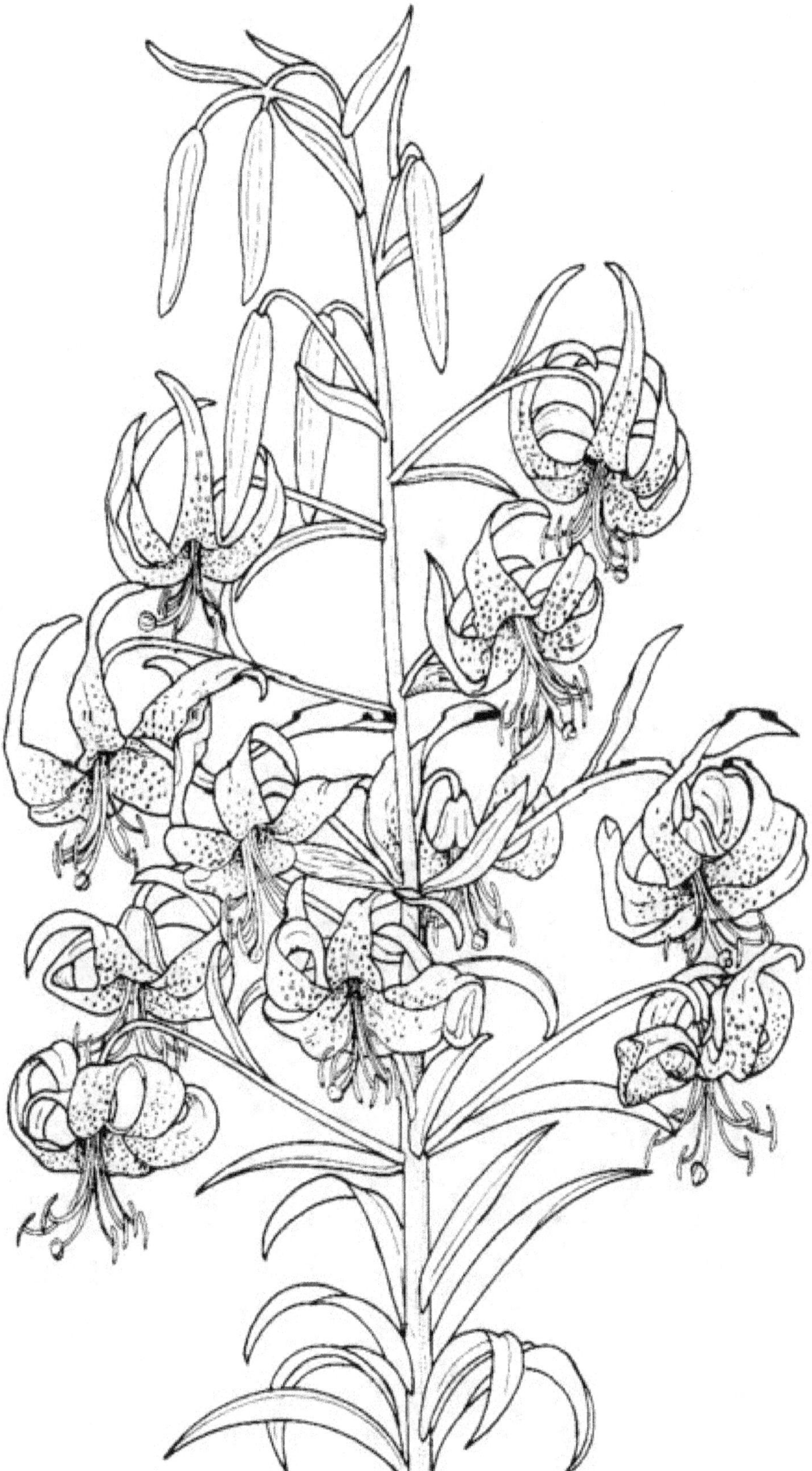

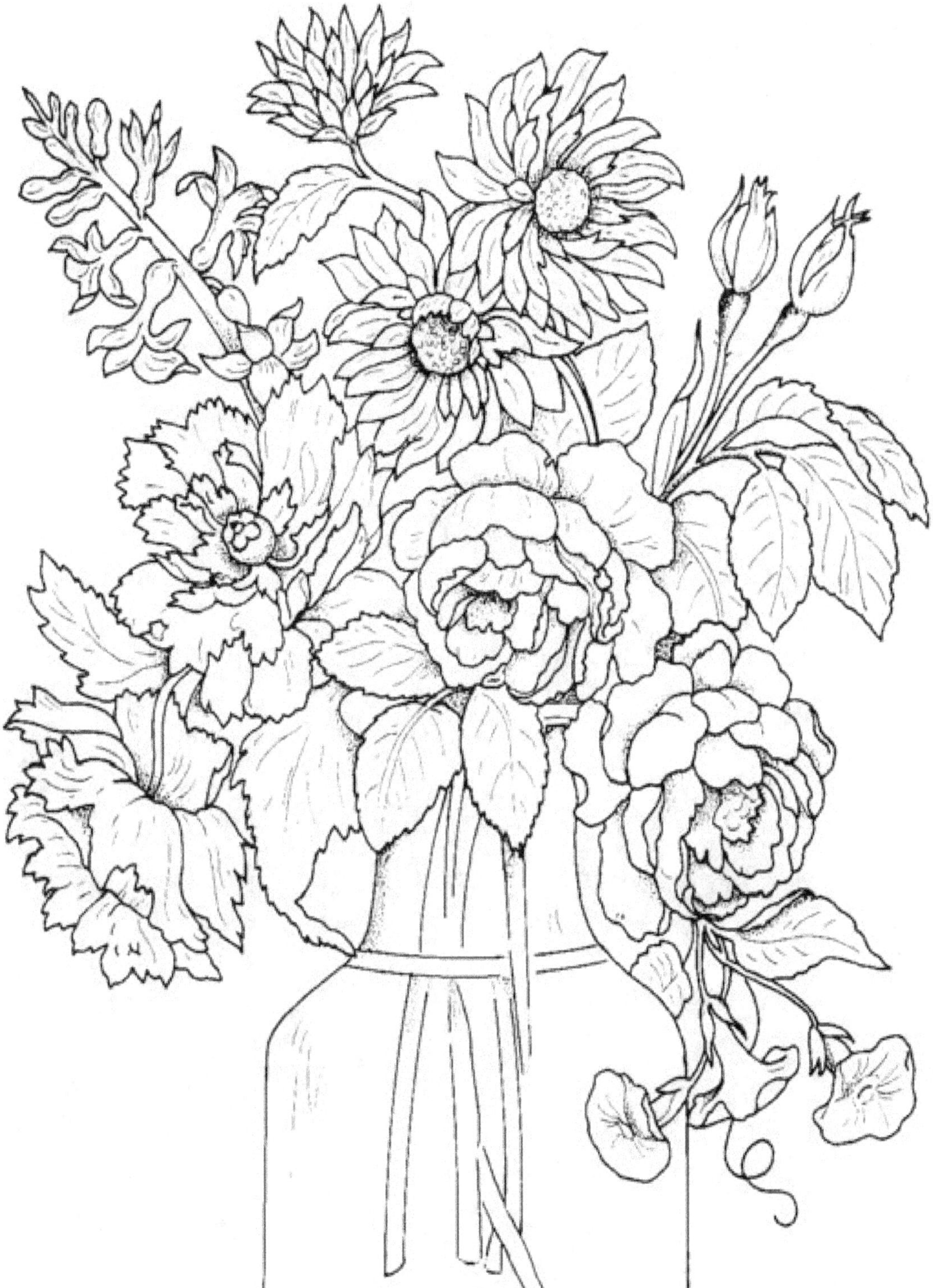

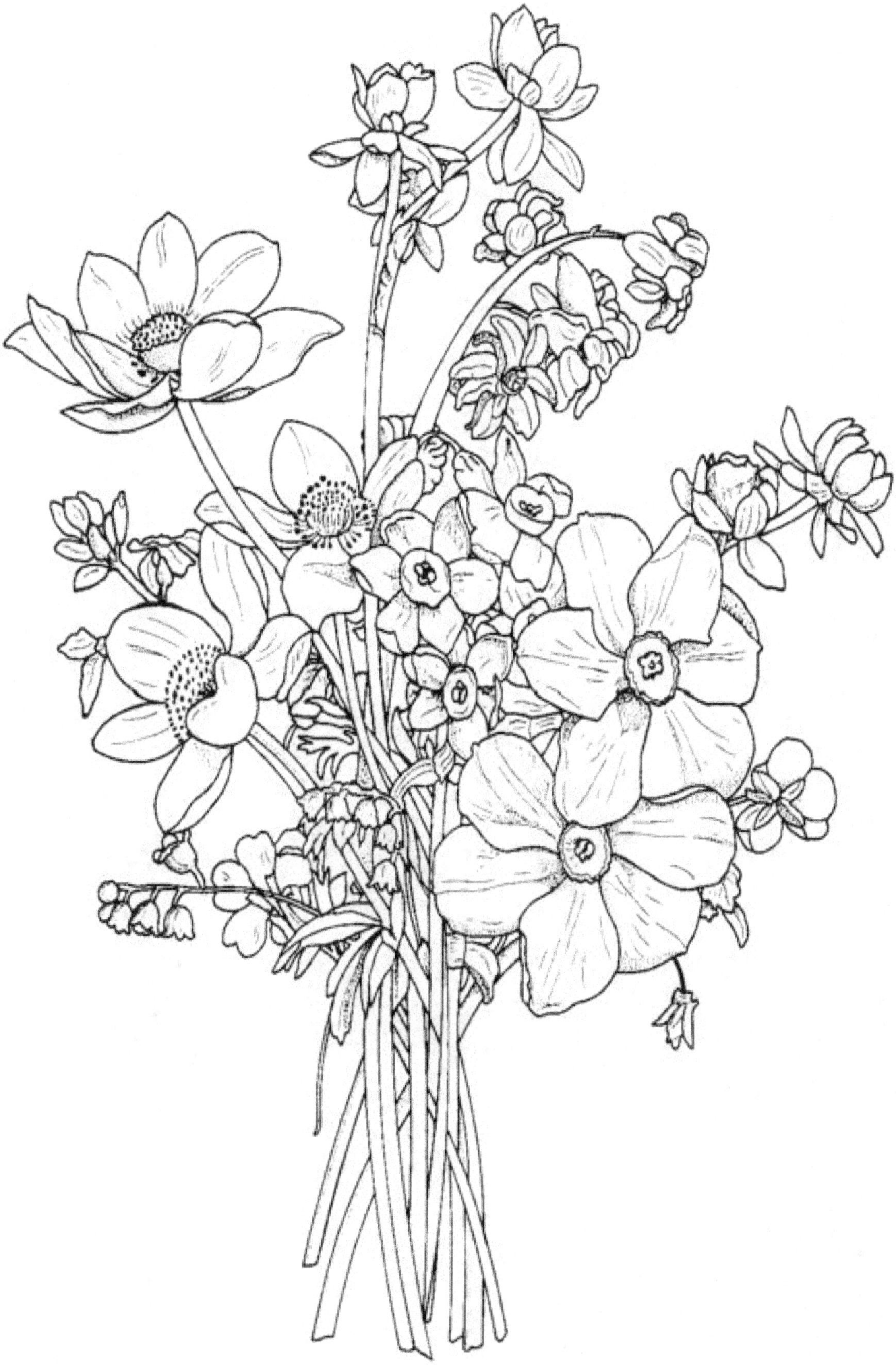

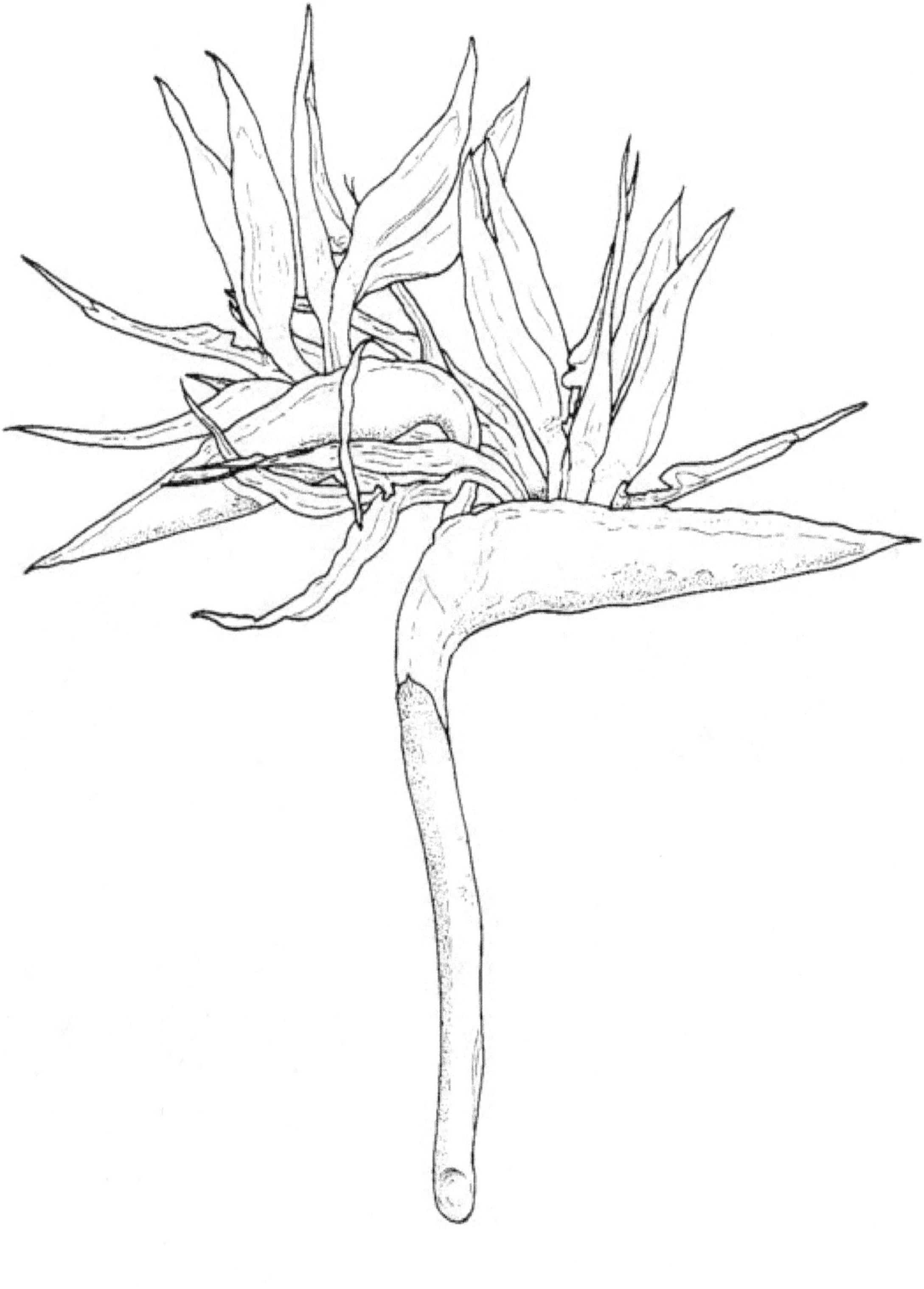

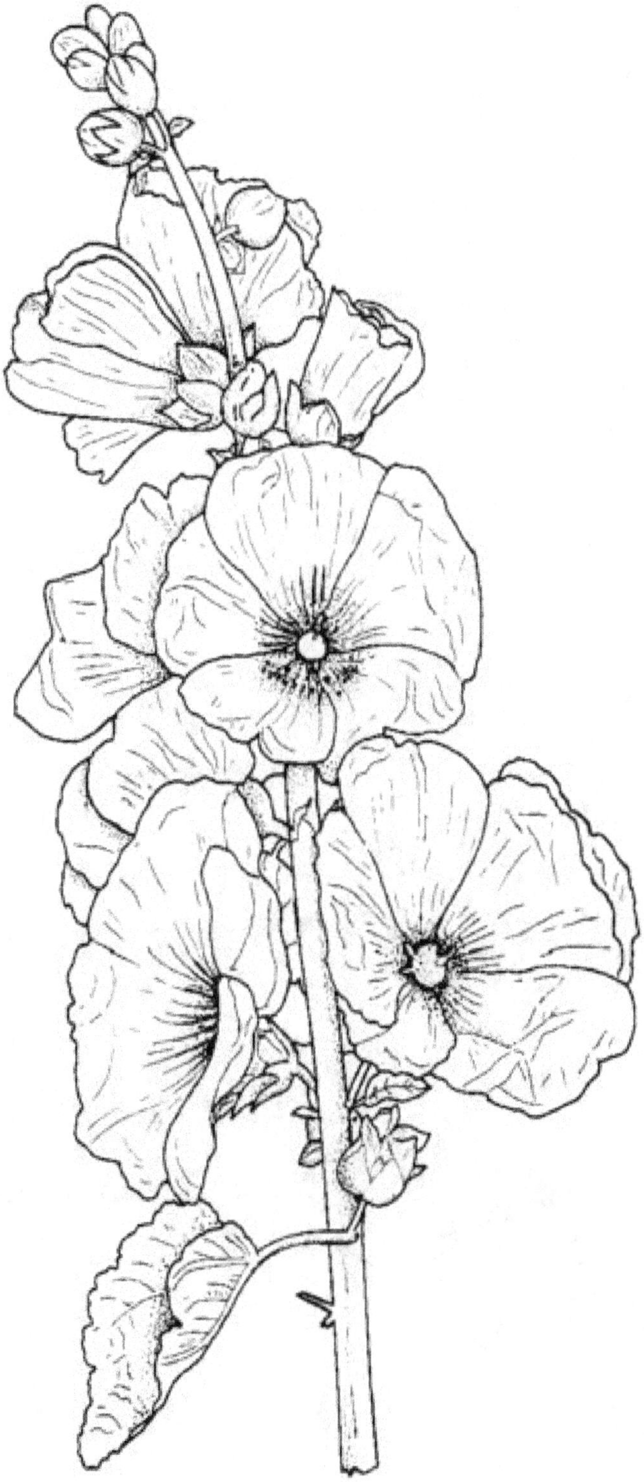

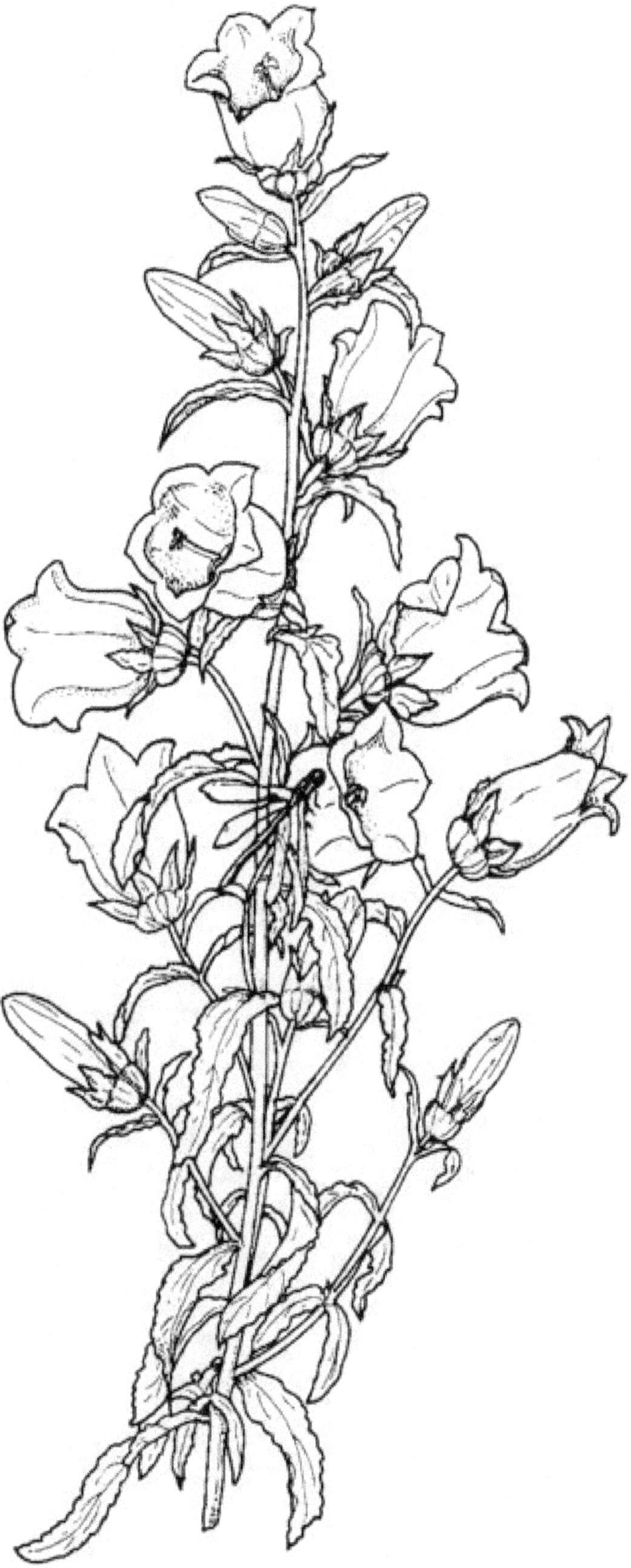

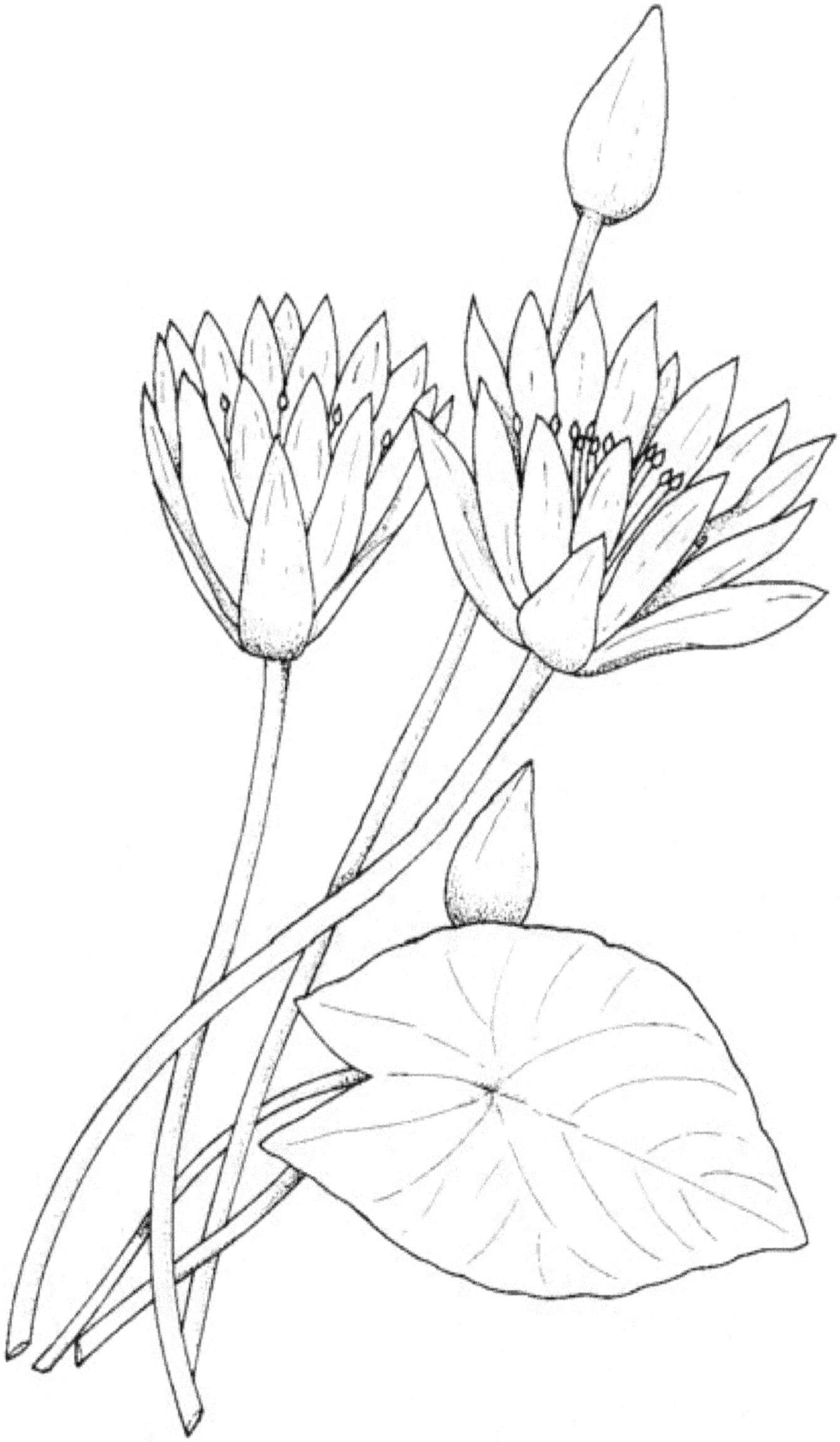

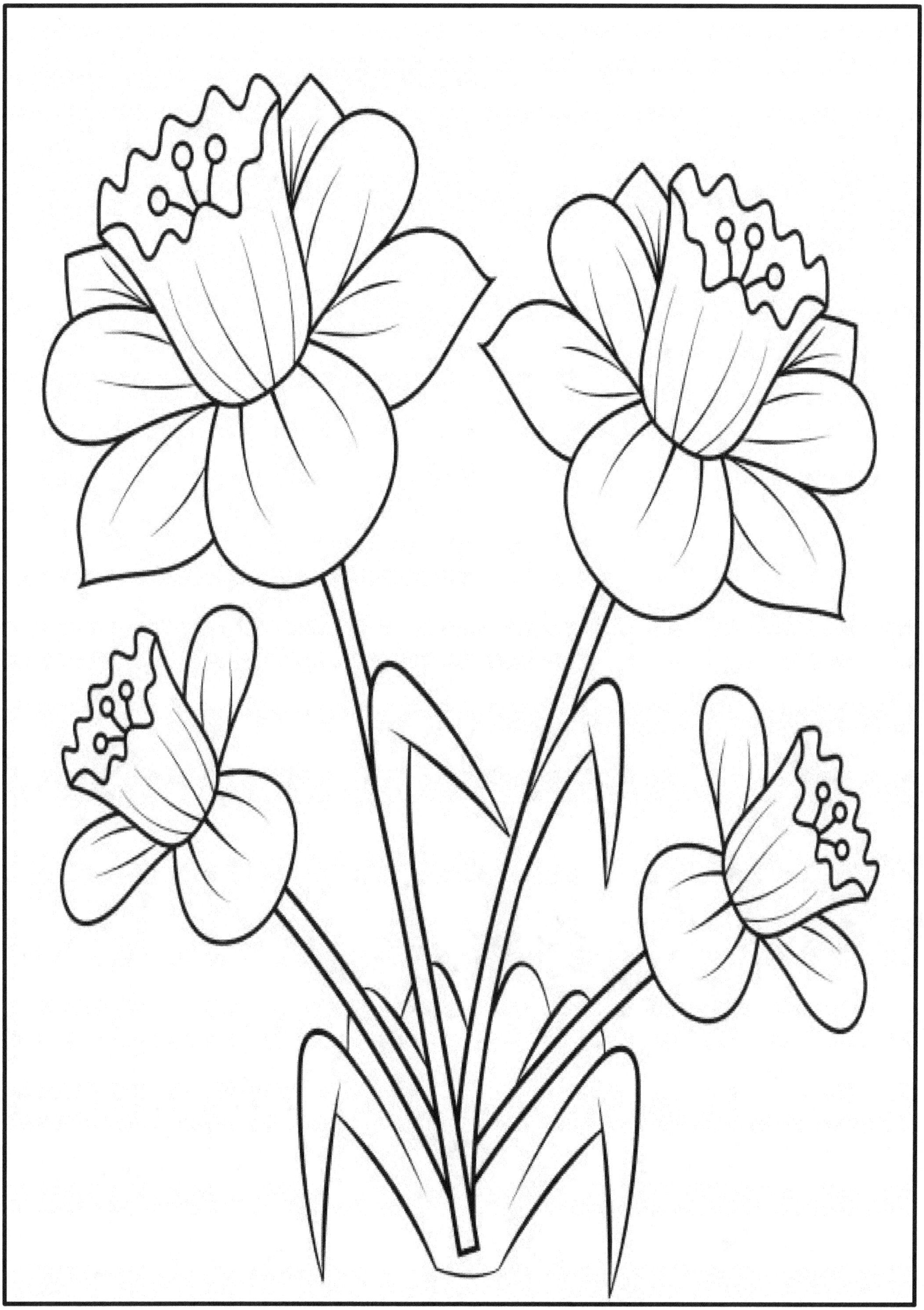

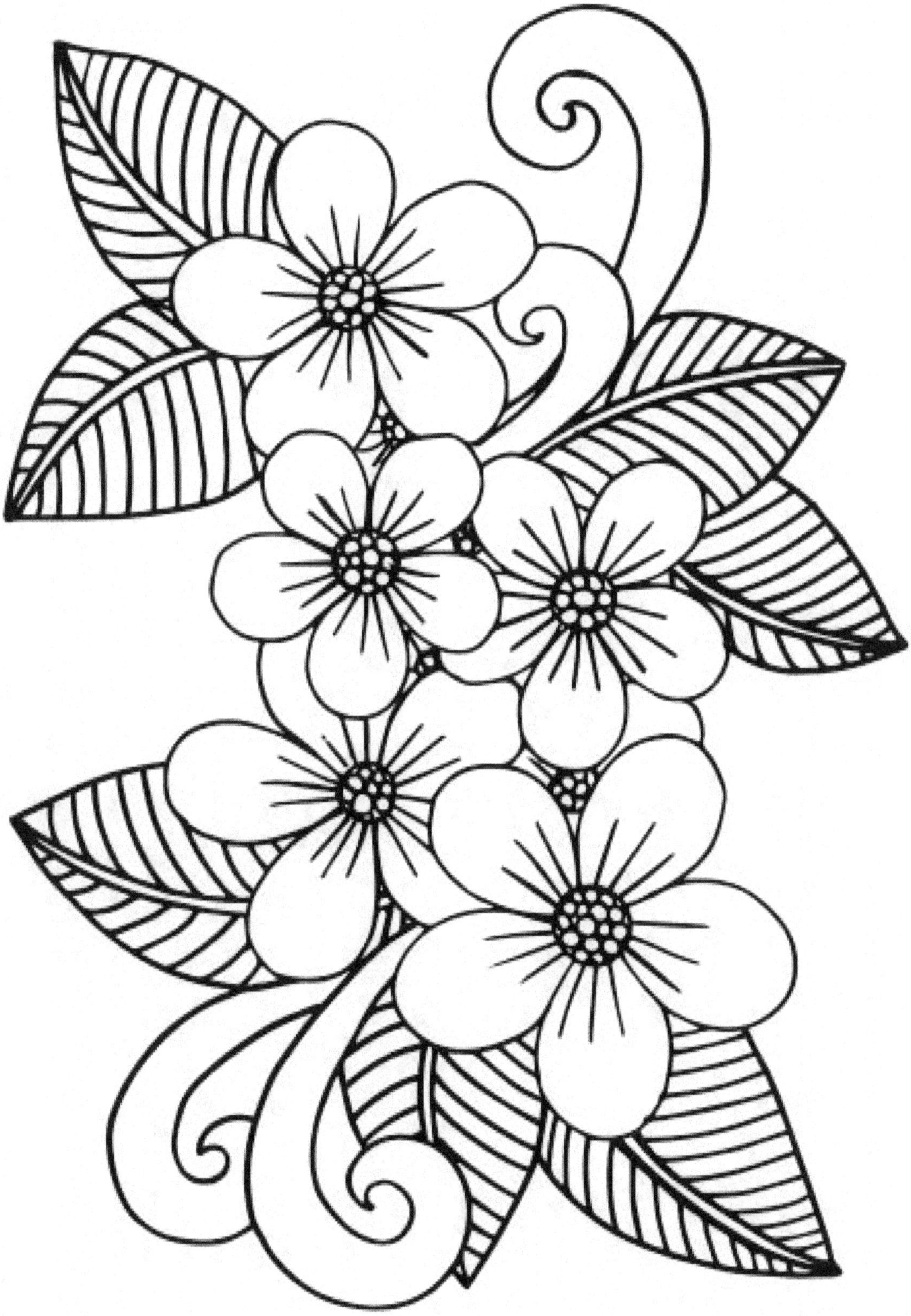

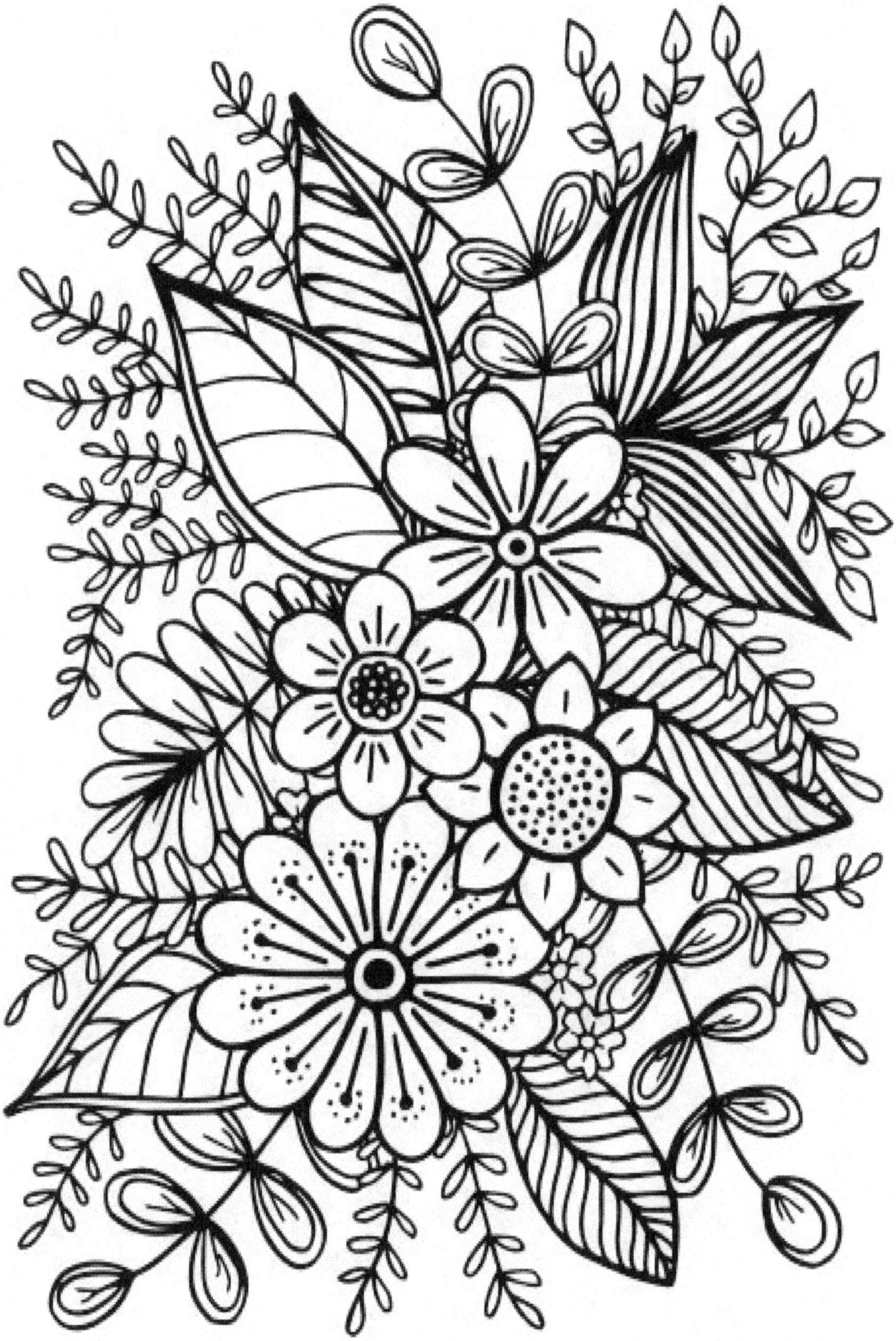

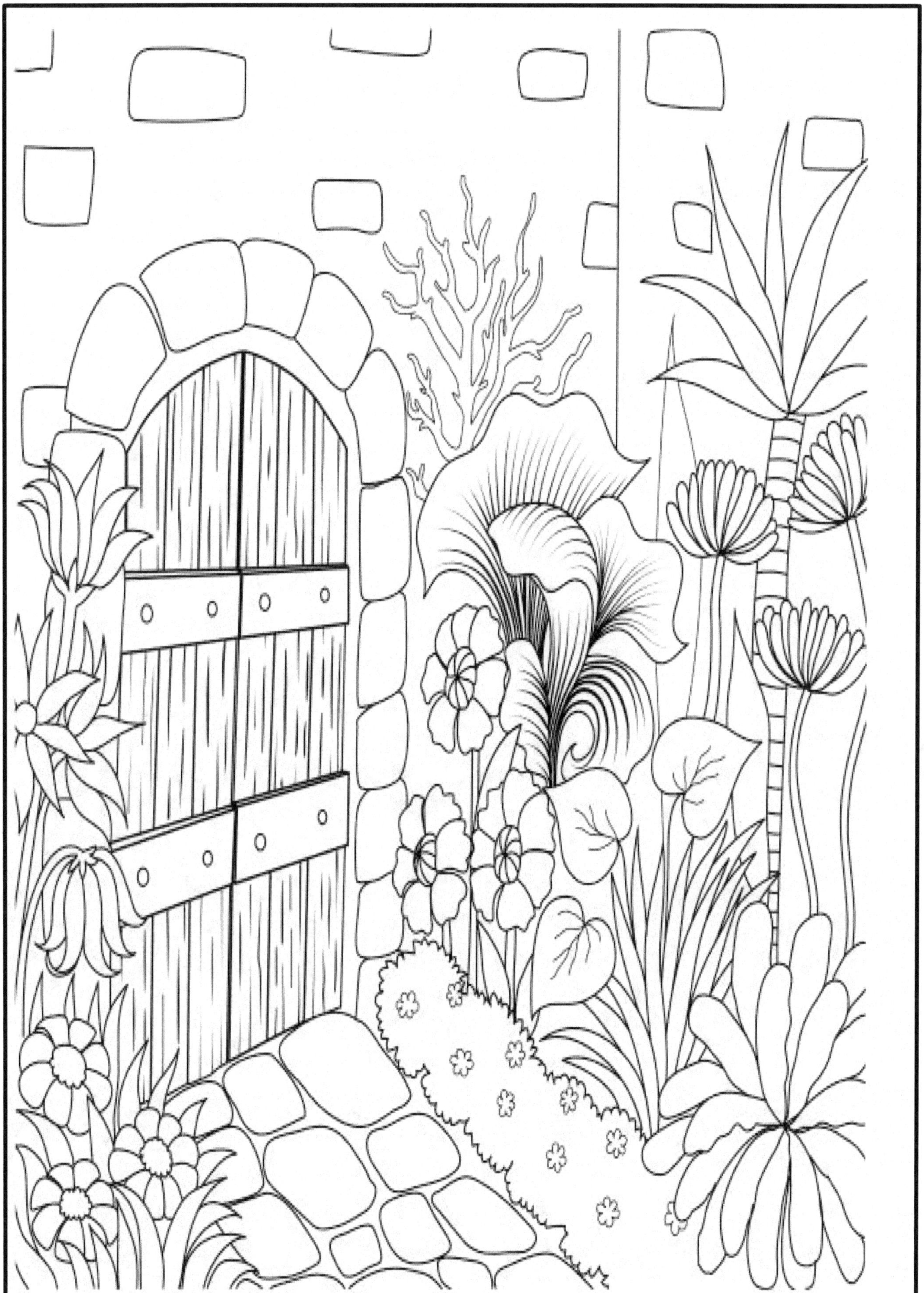

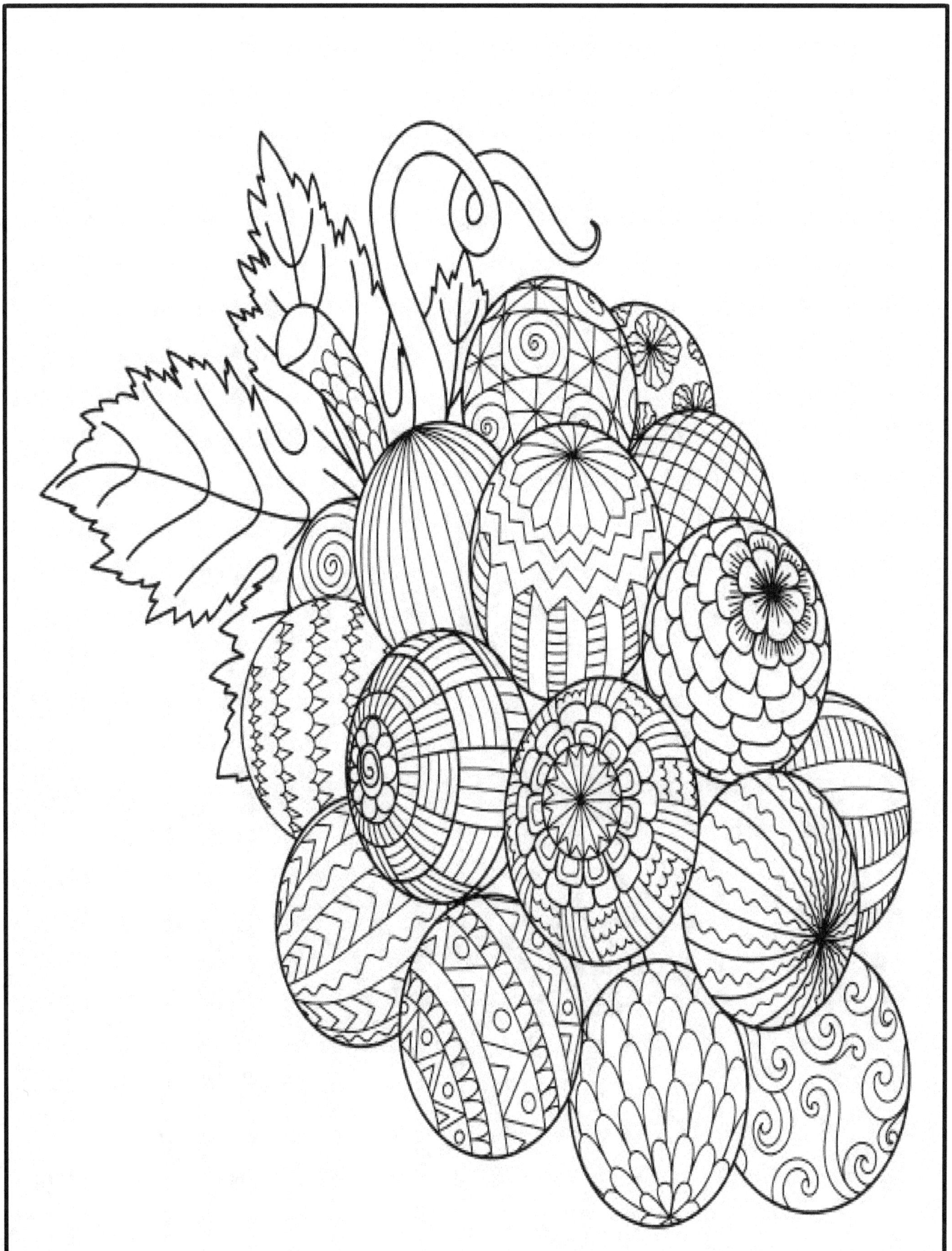

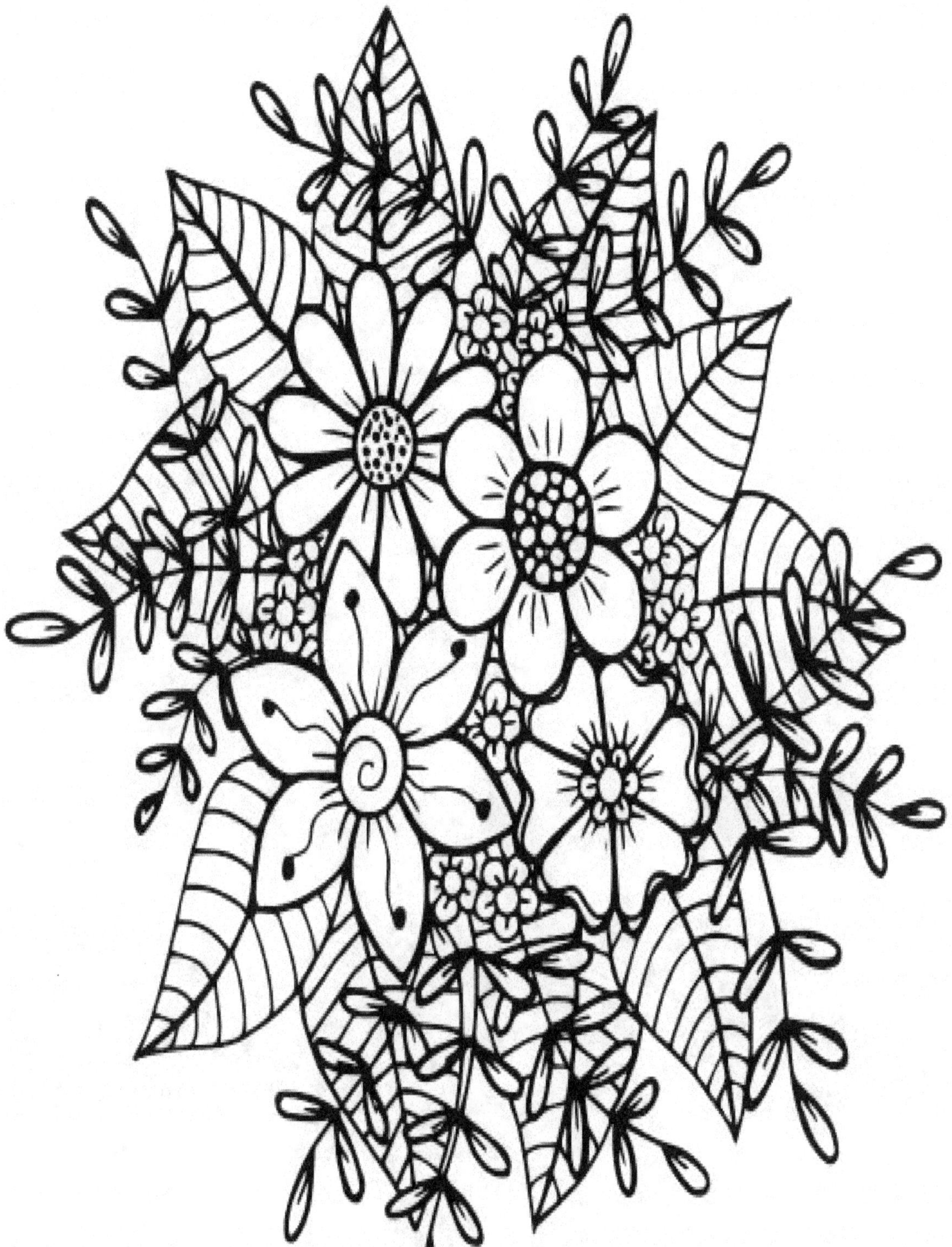

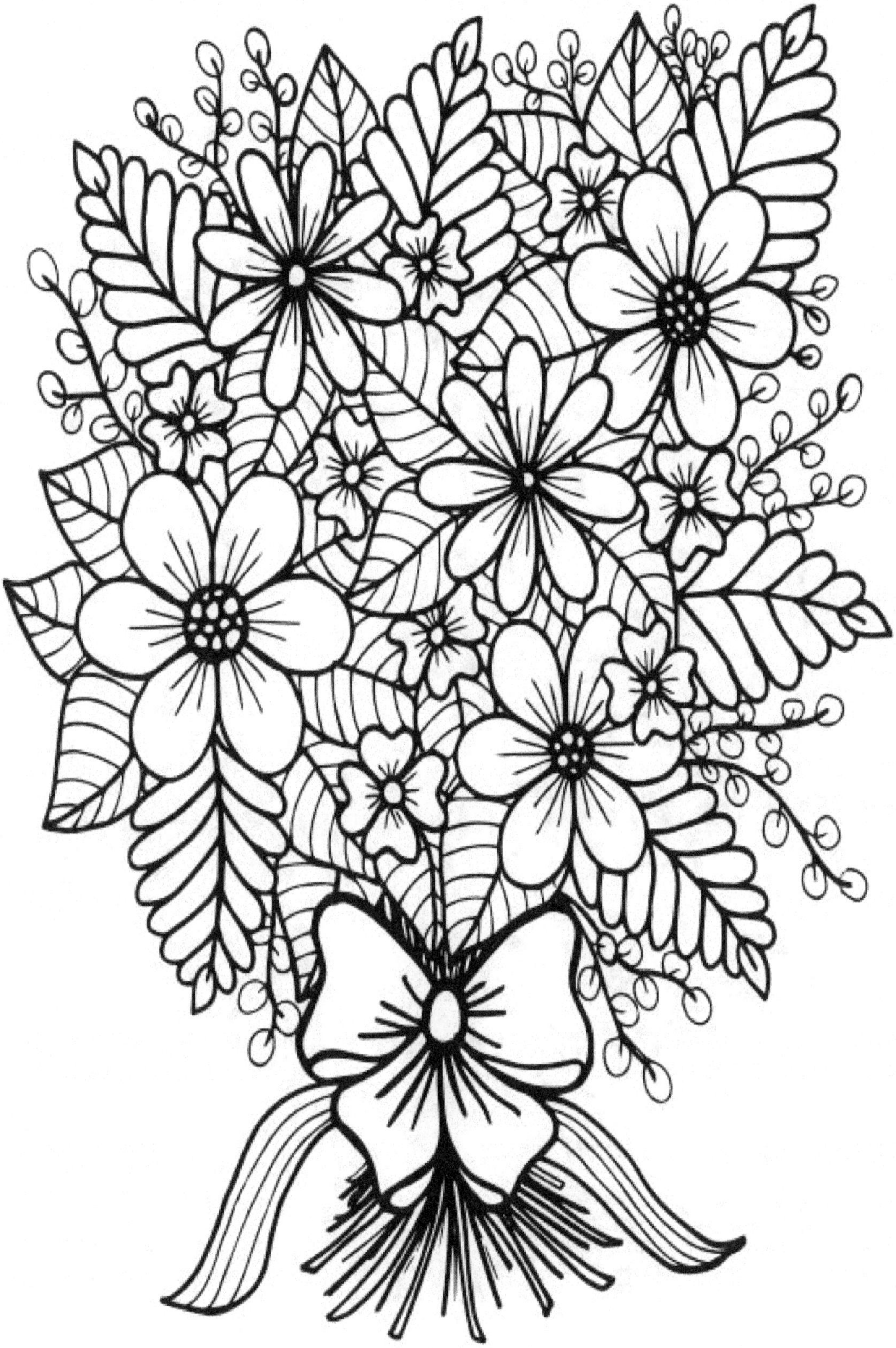

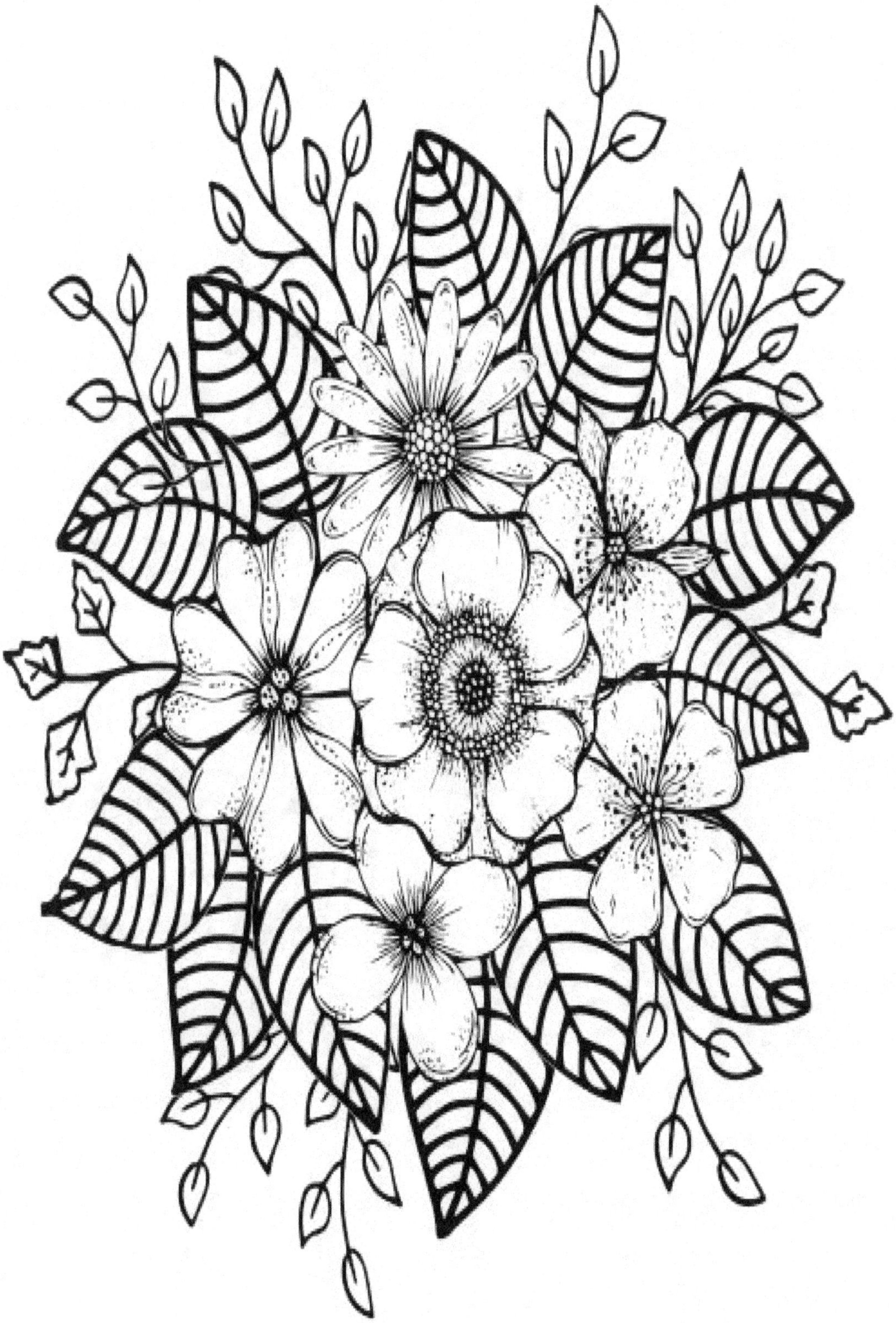

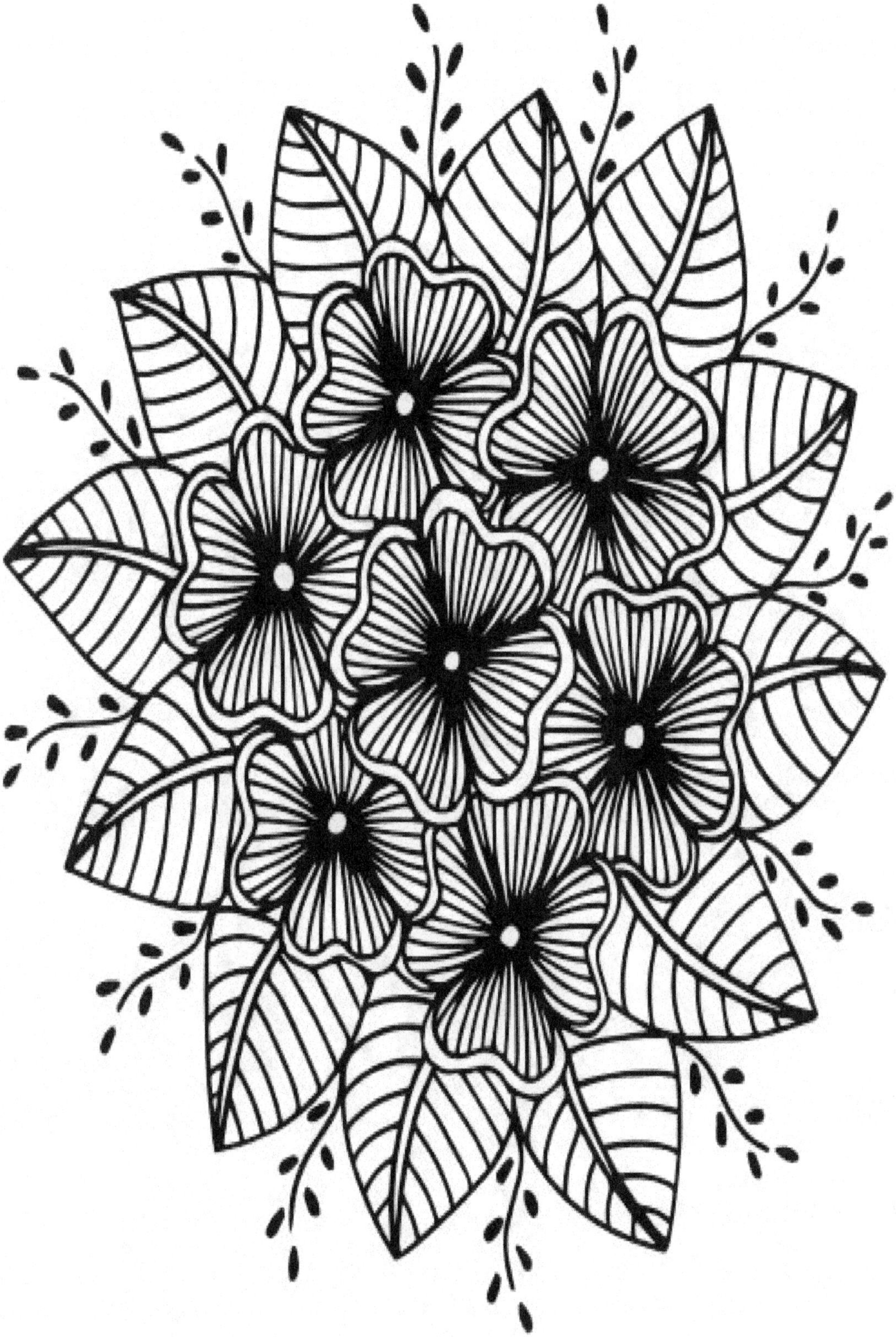

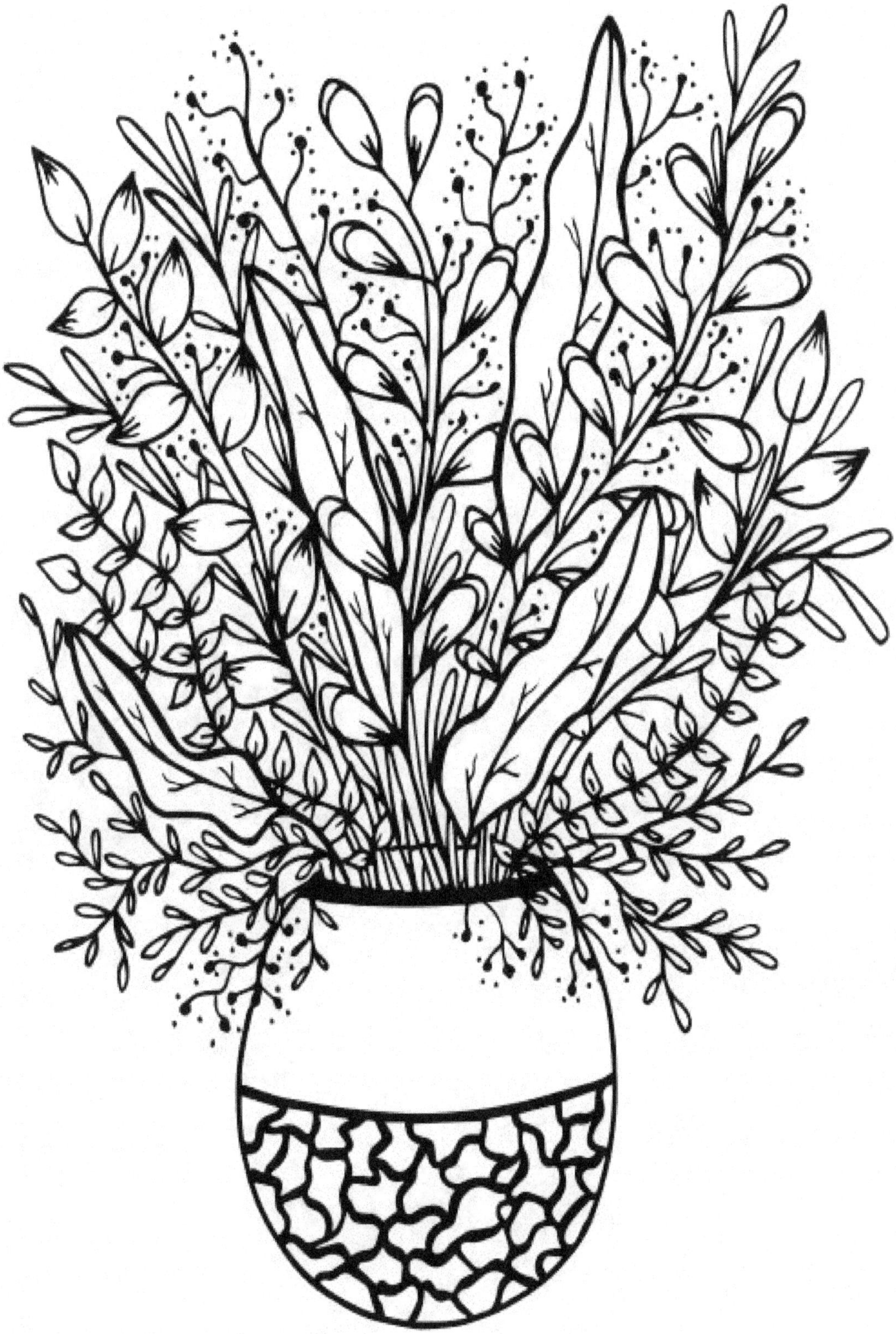

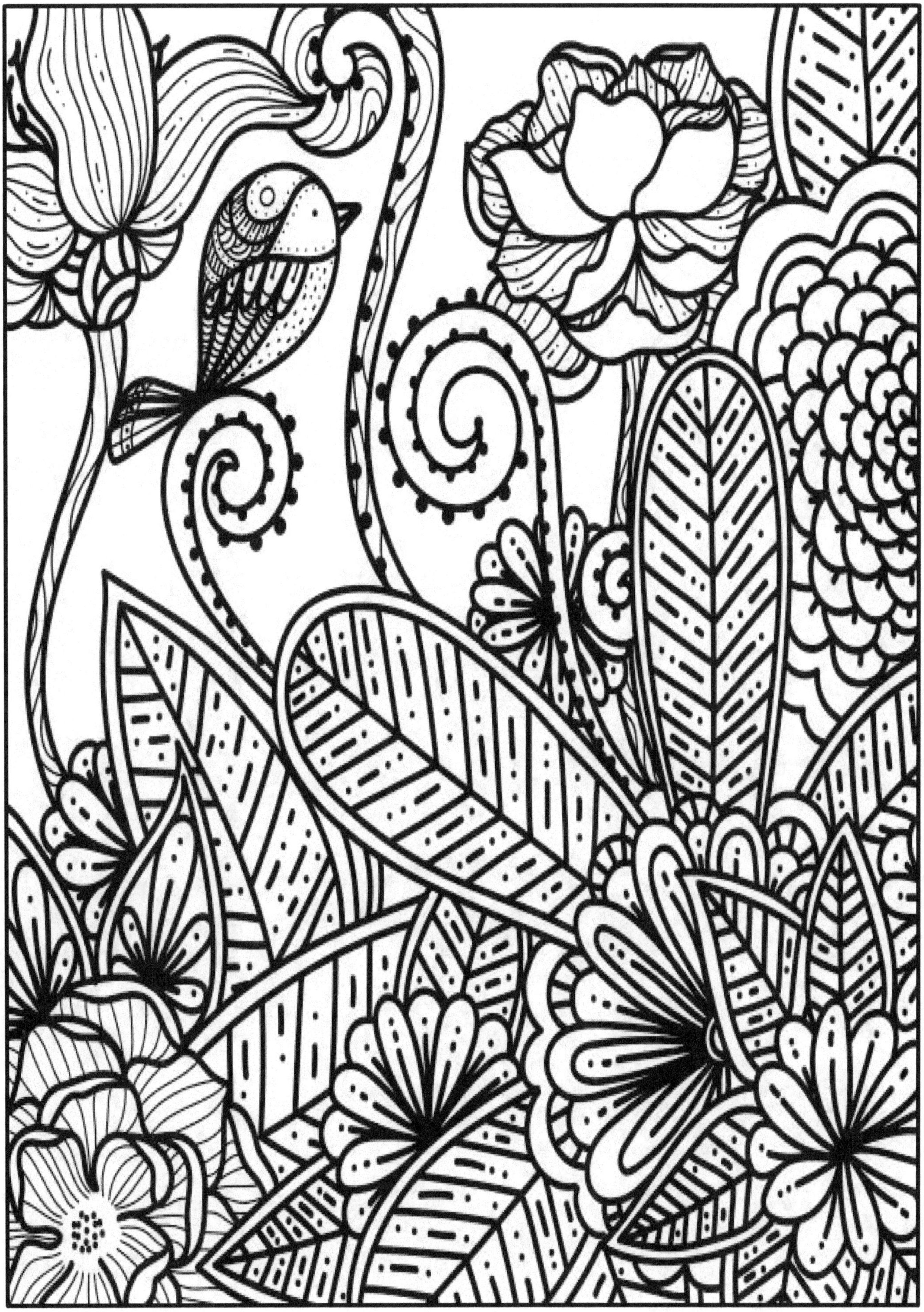

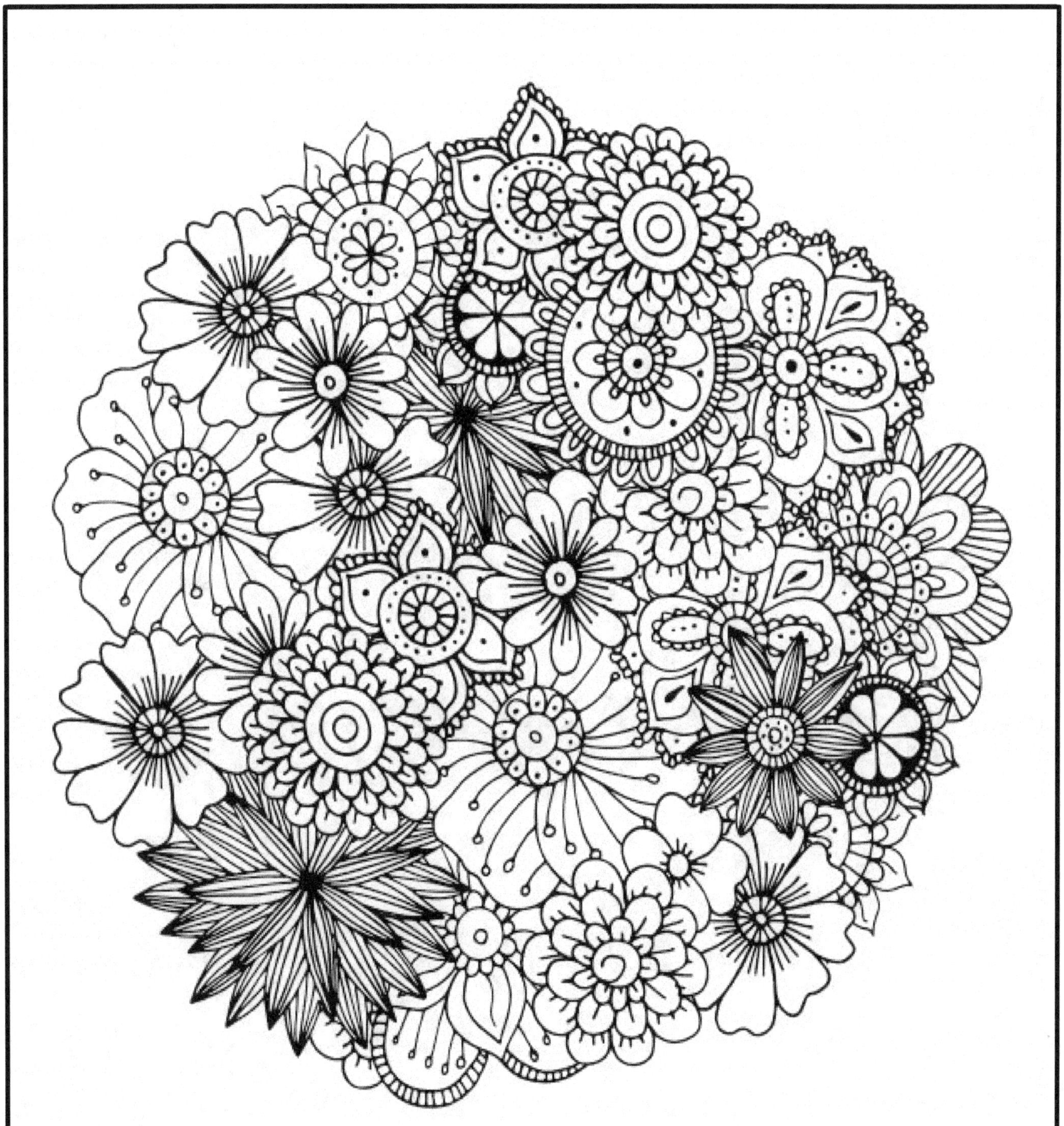

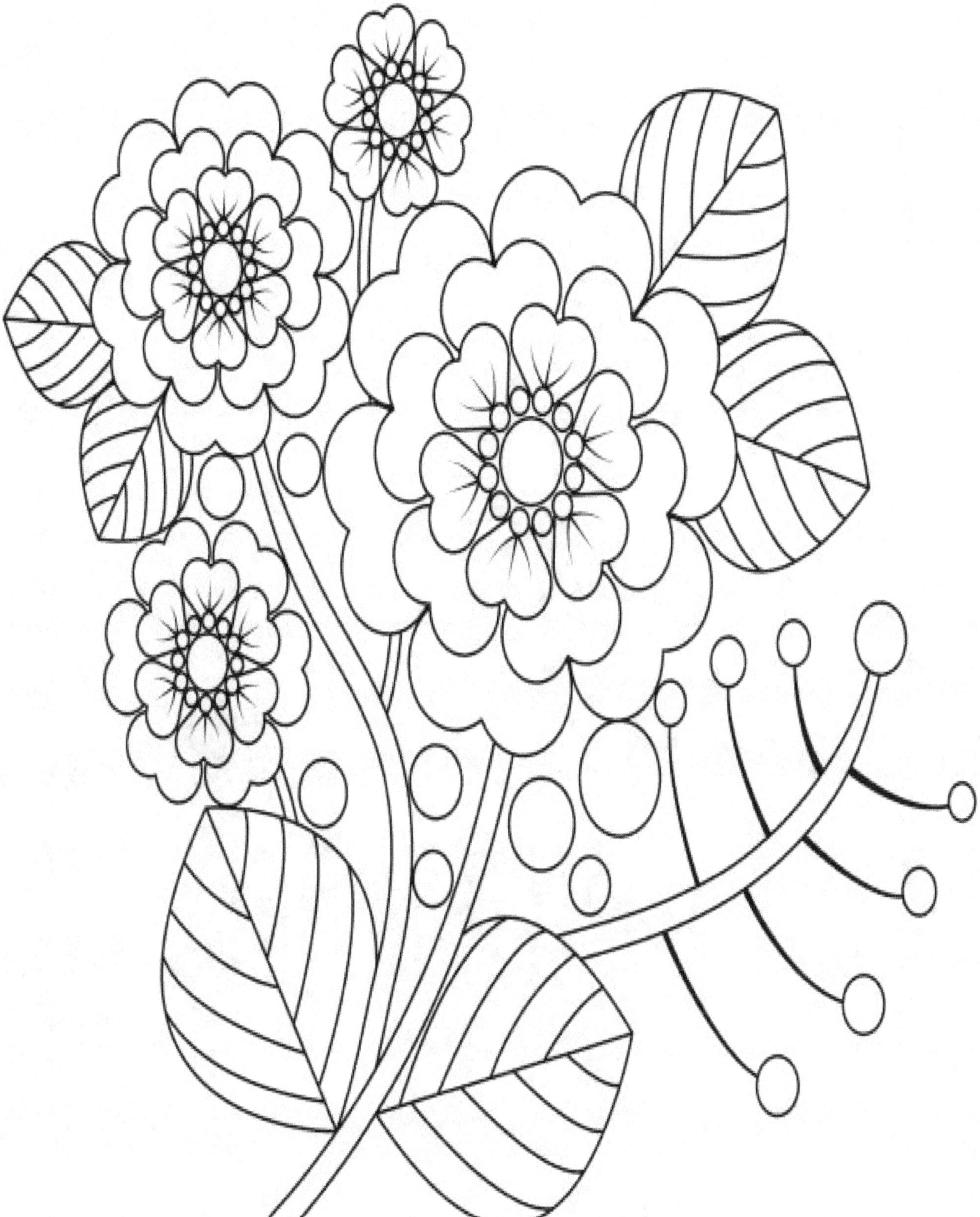

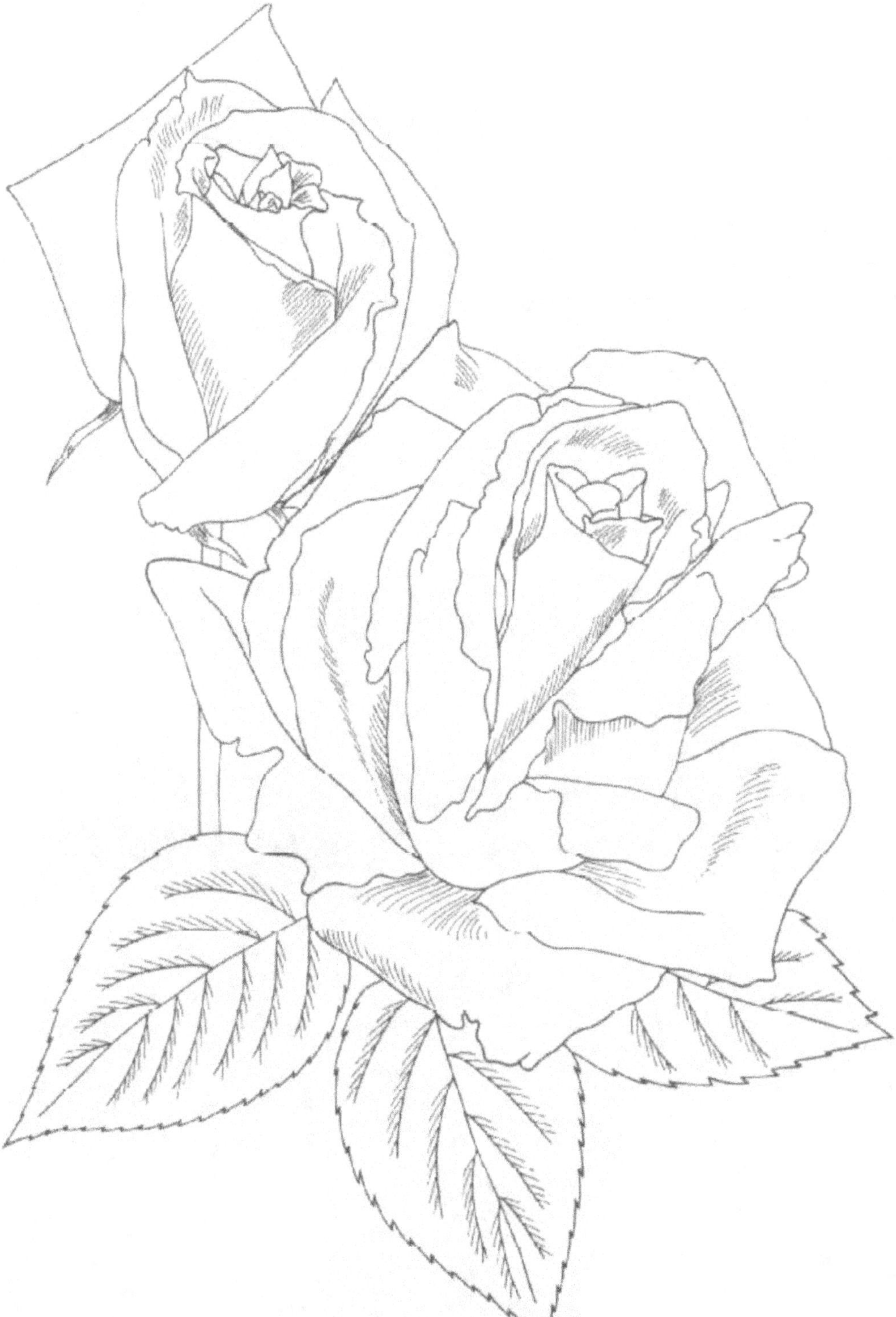

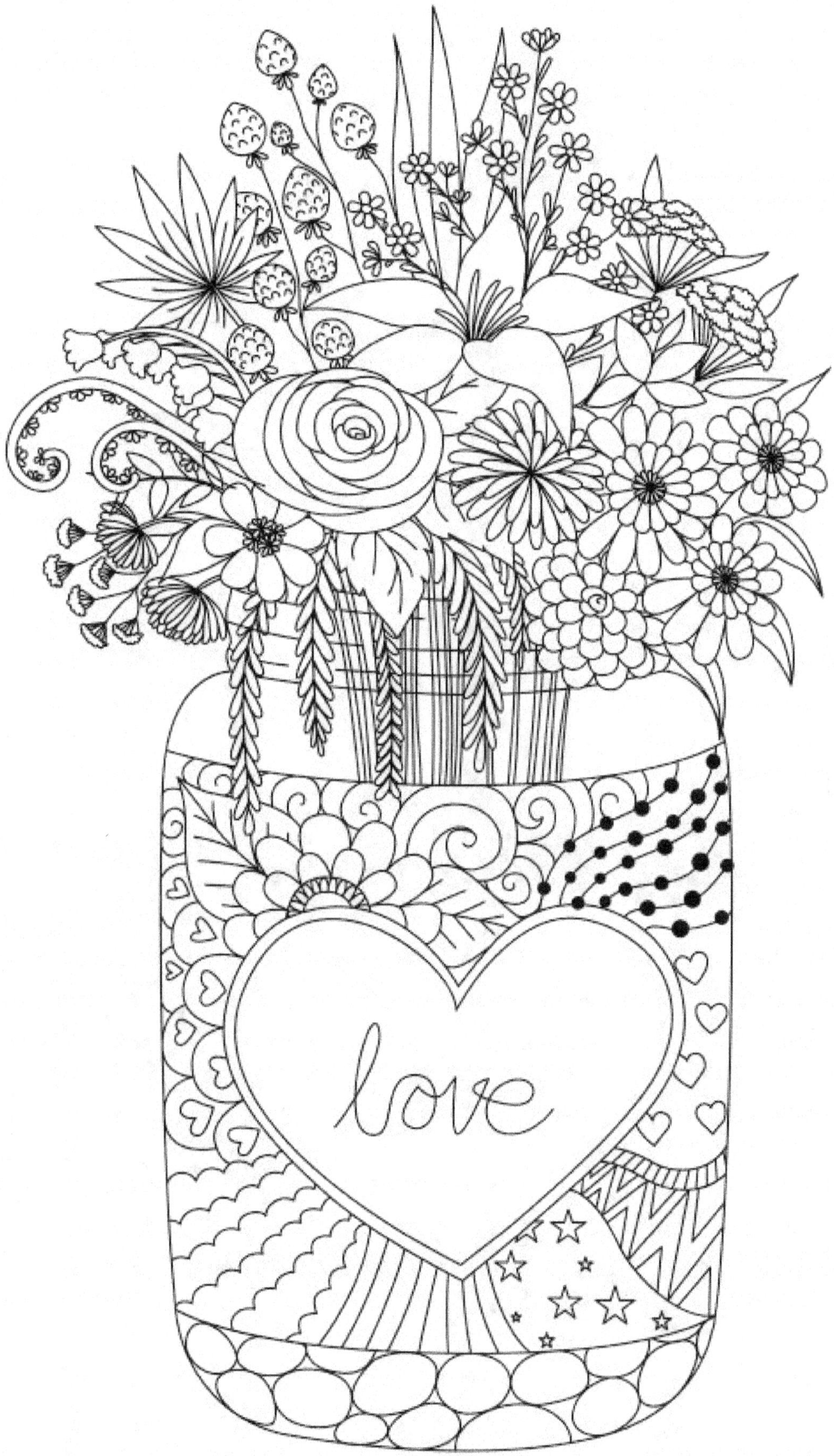
love

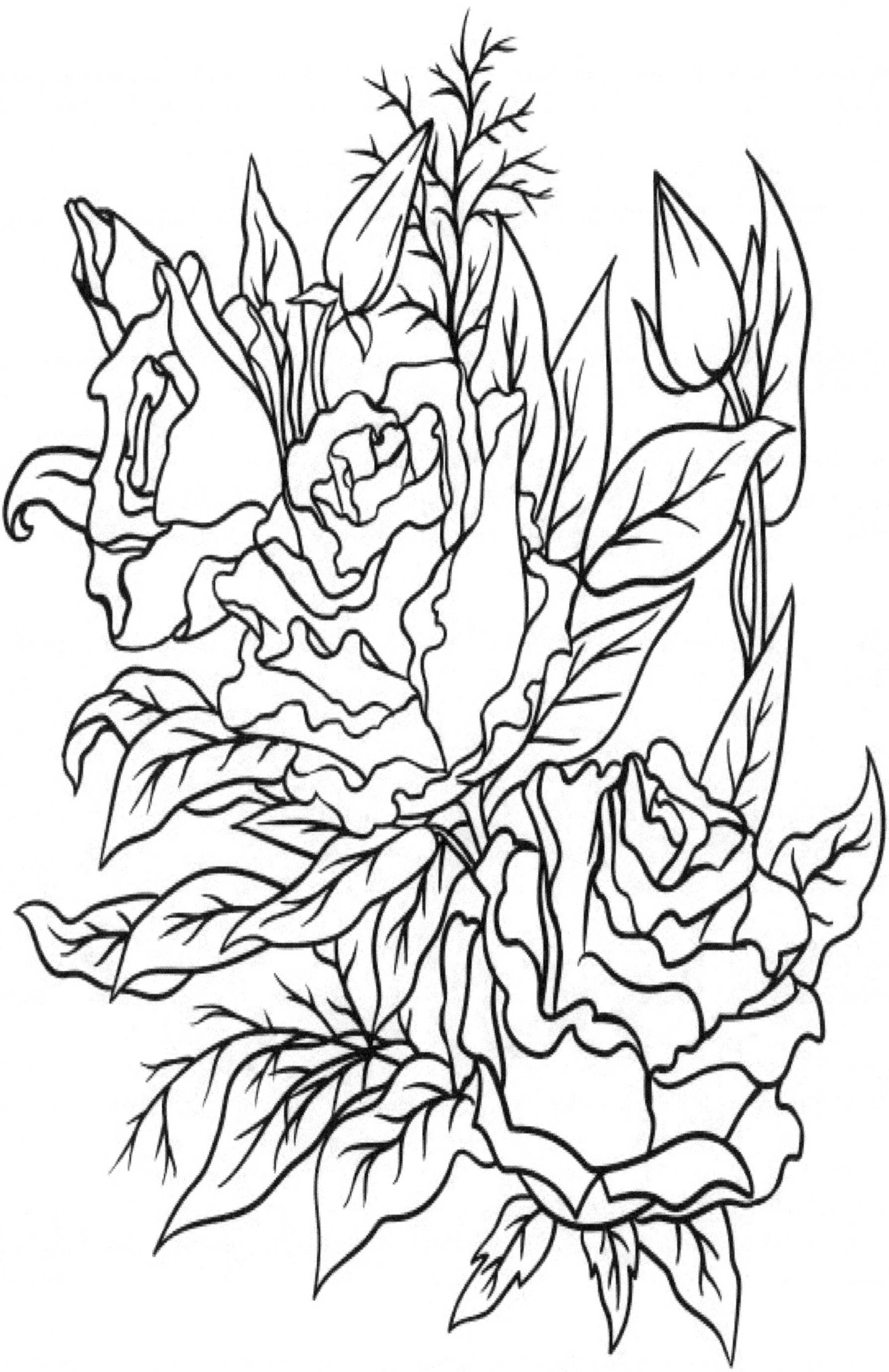

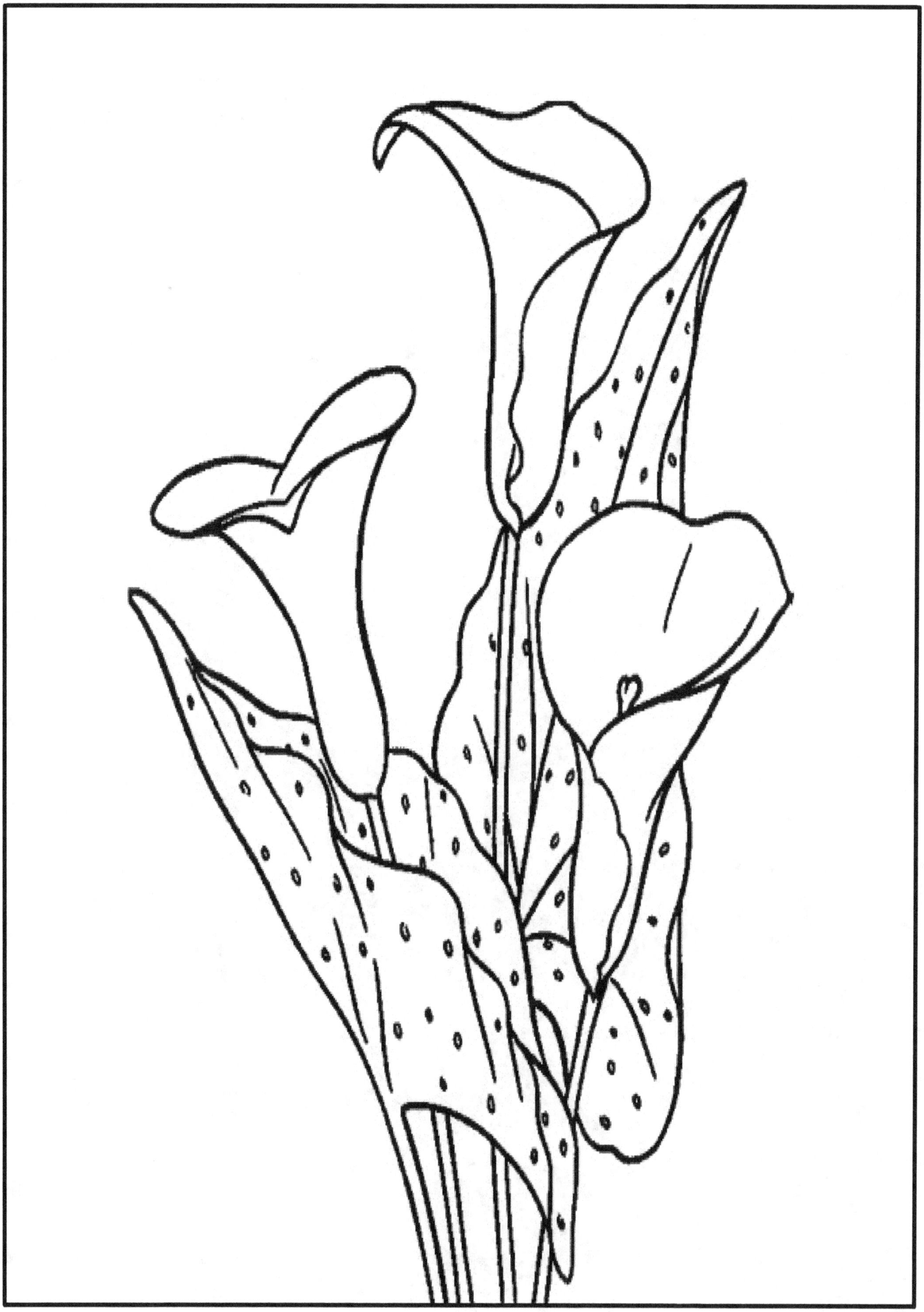

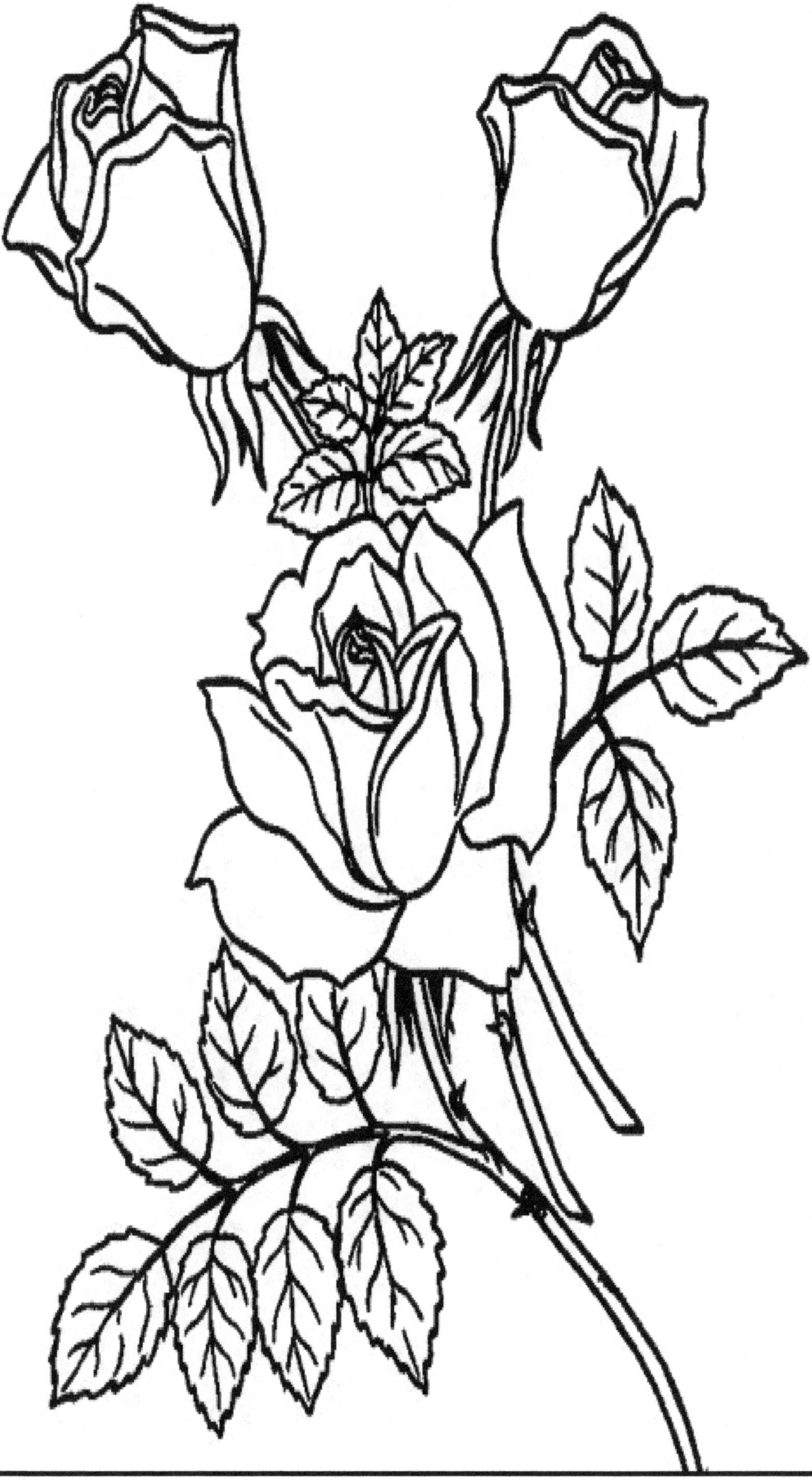

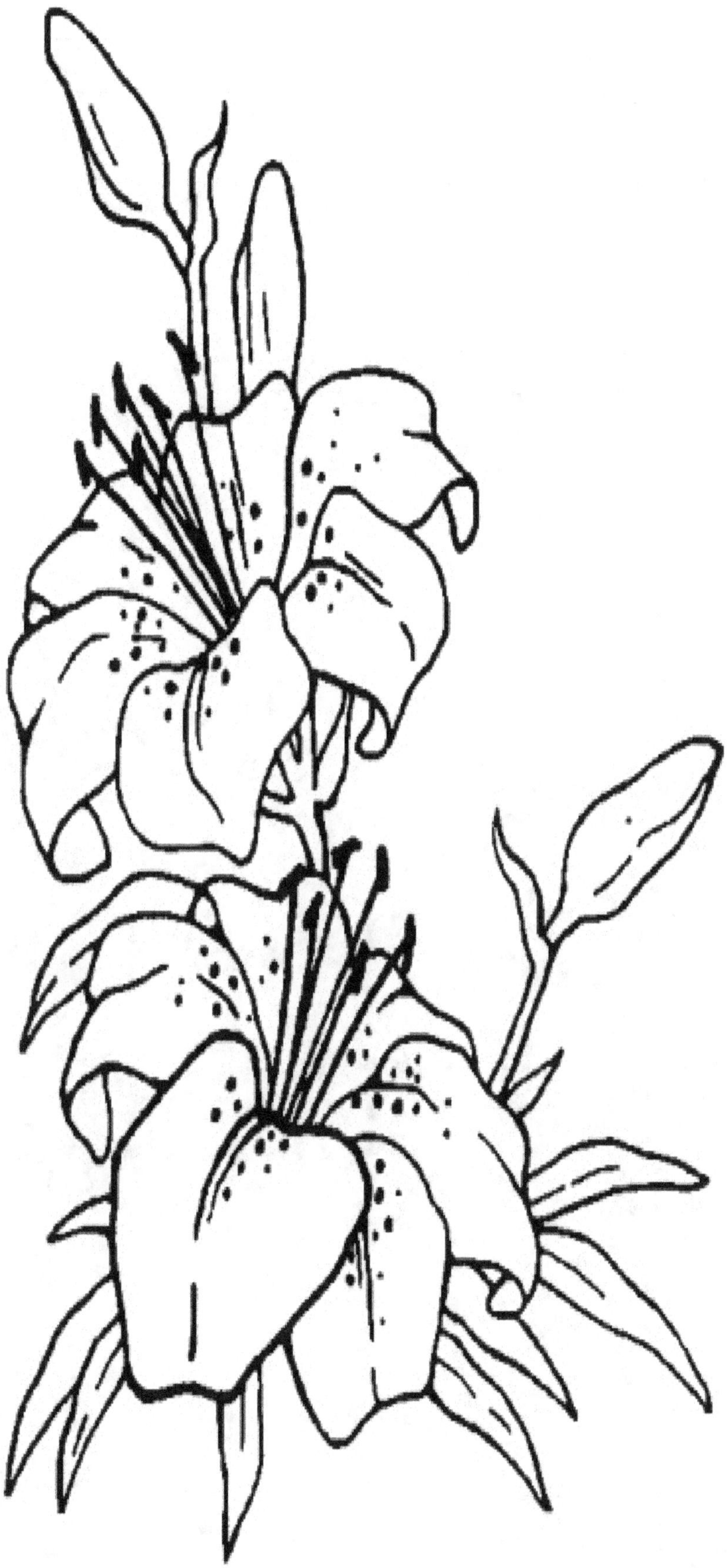

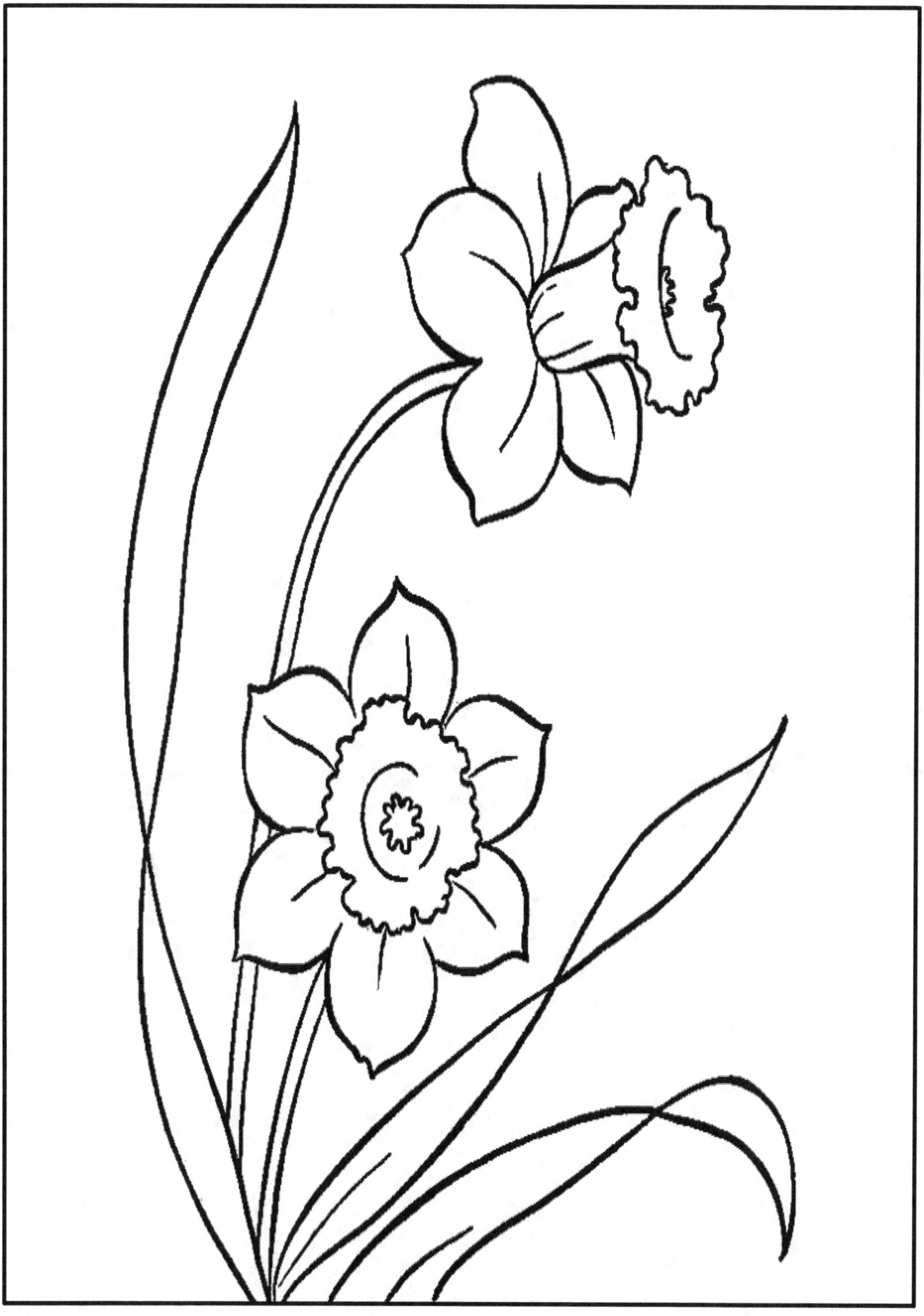

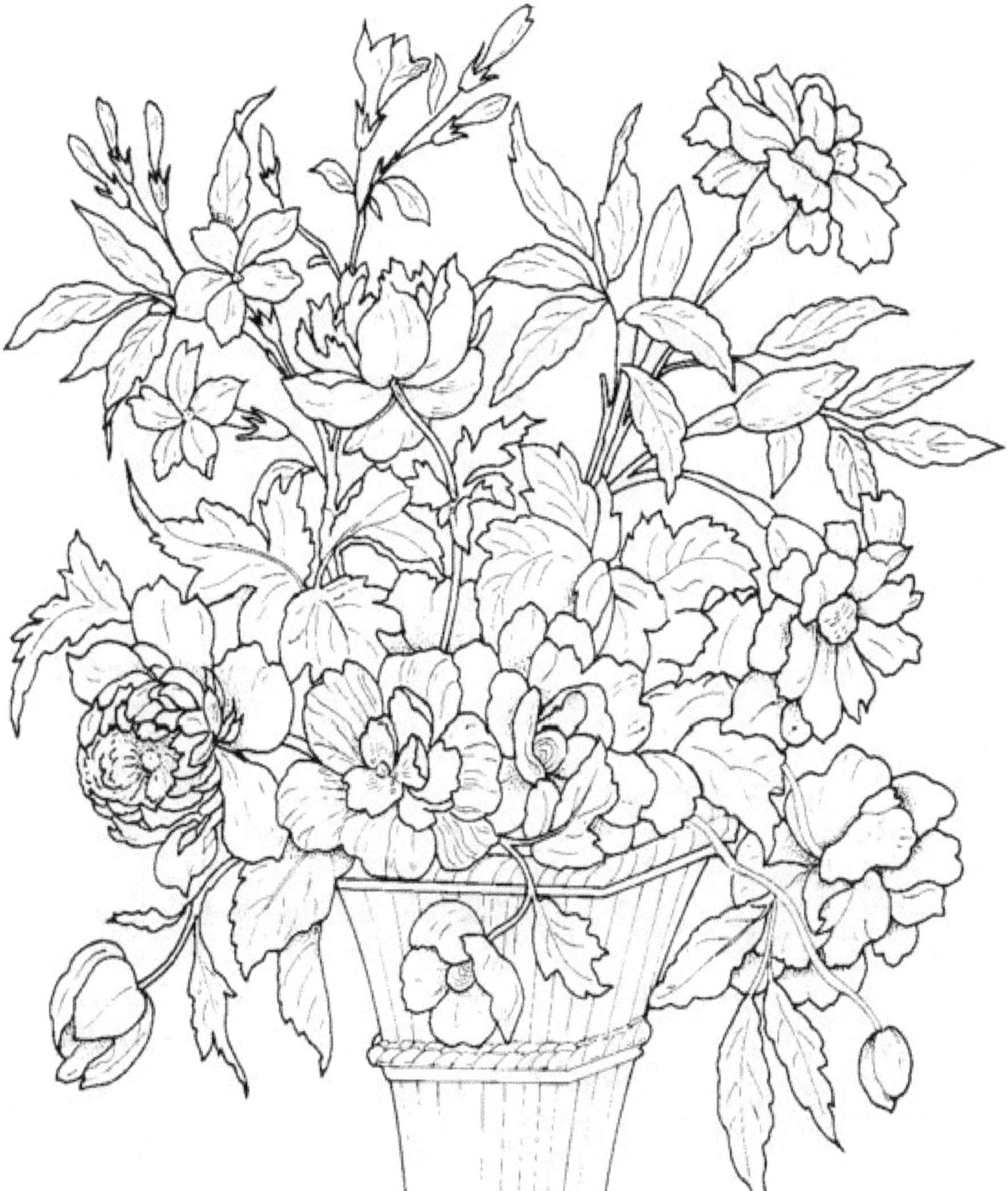

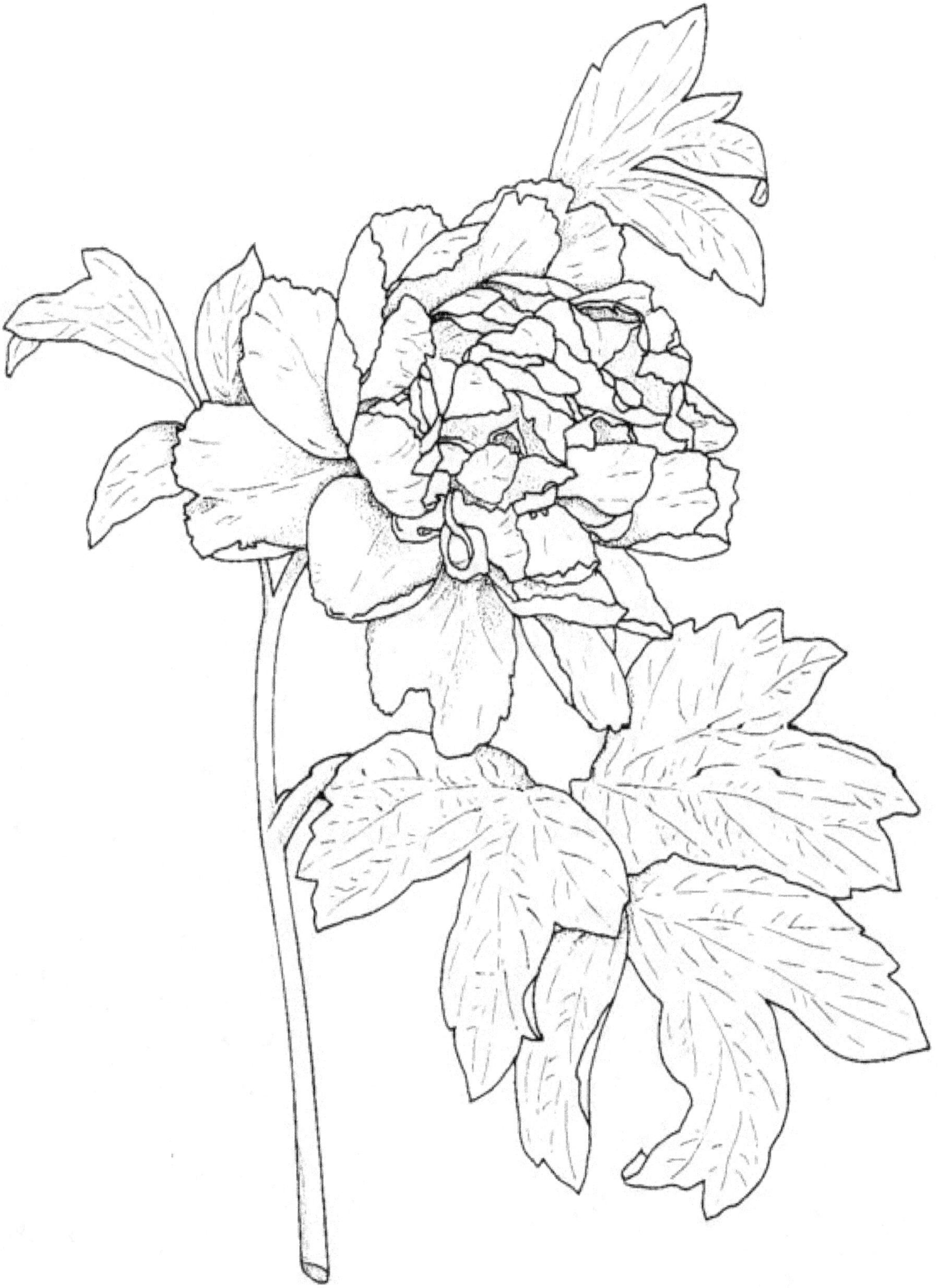

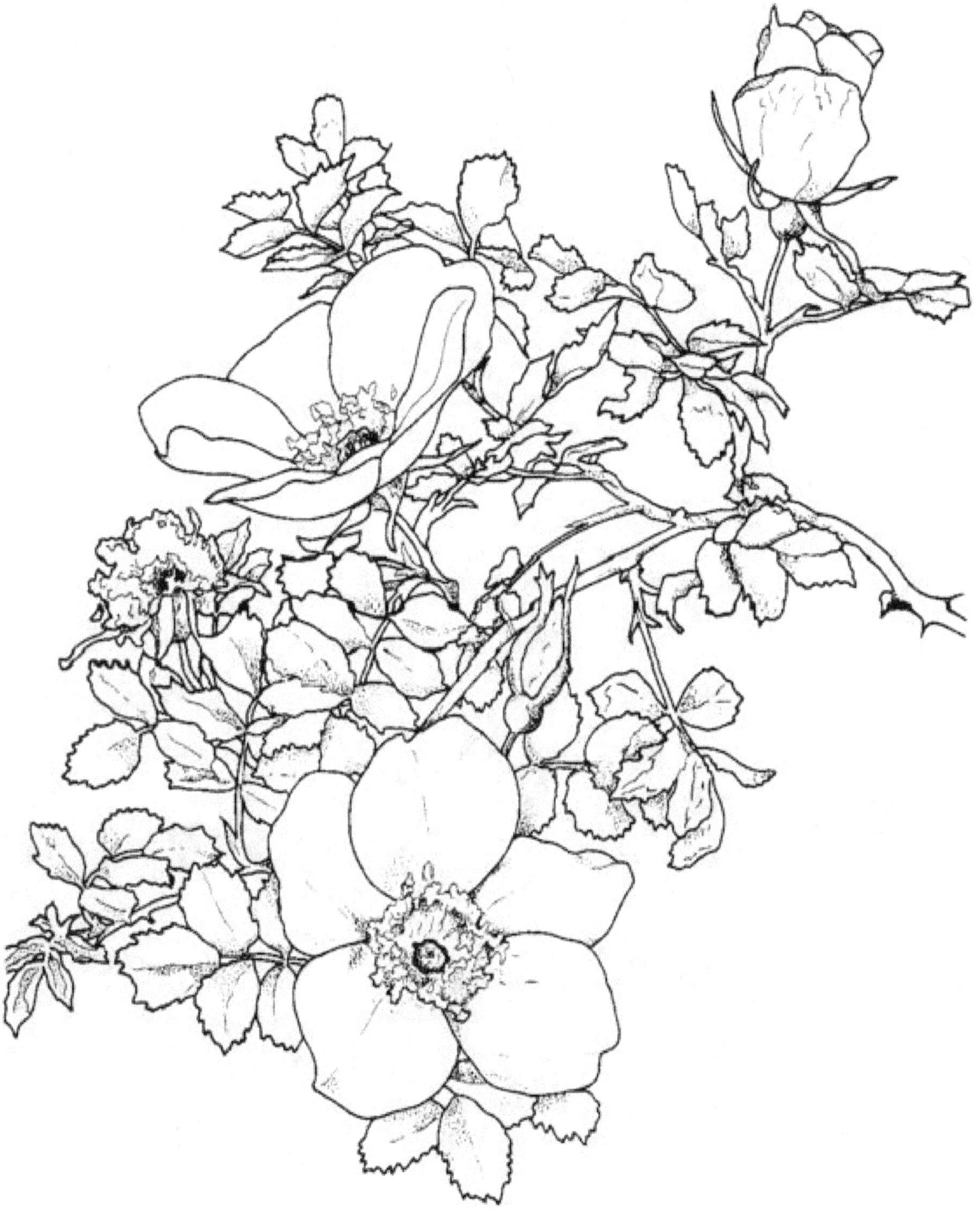

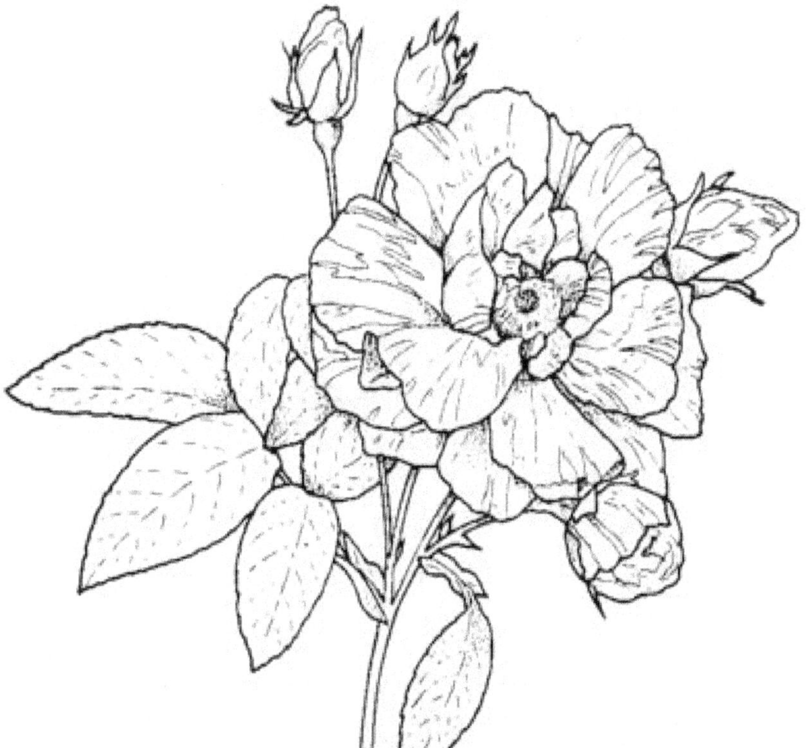

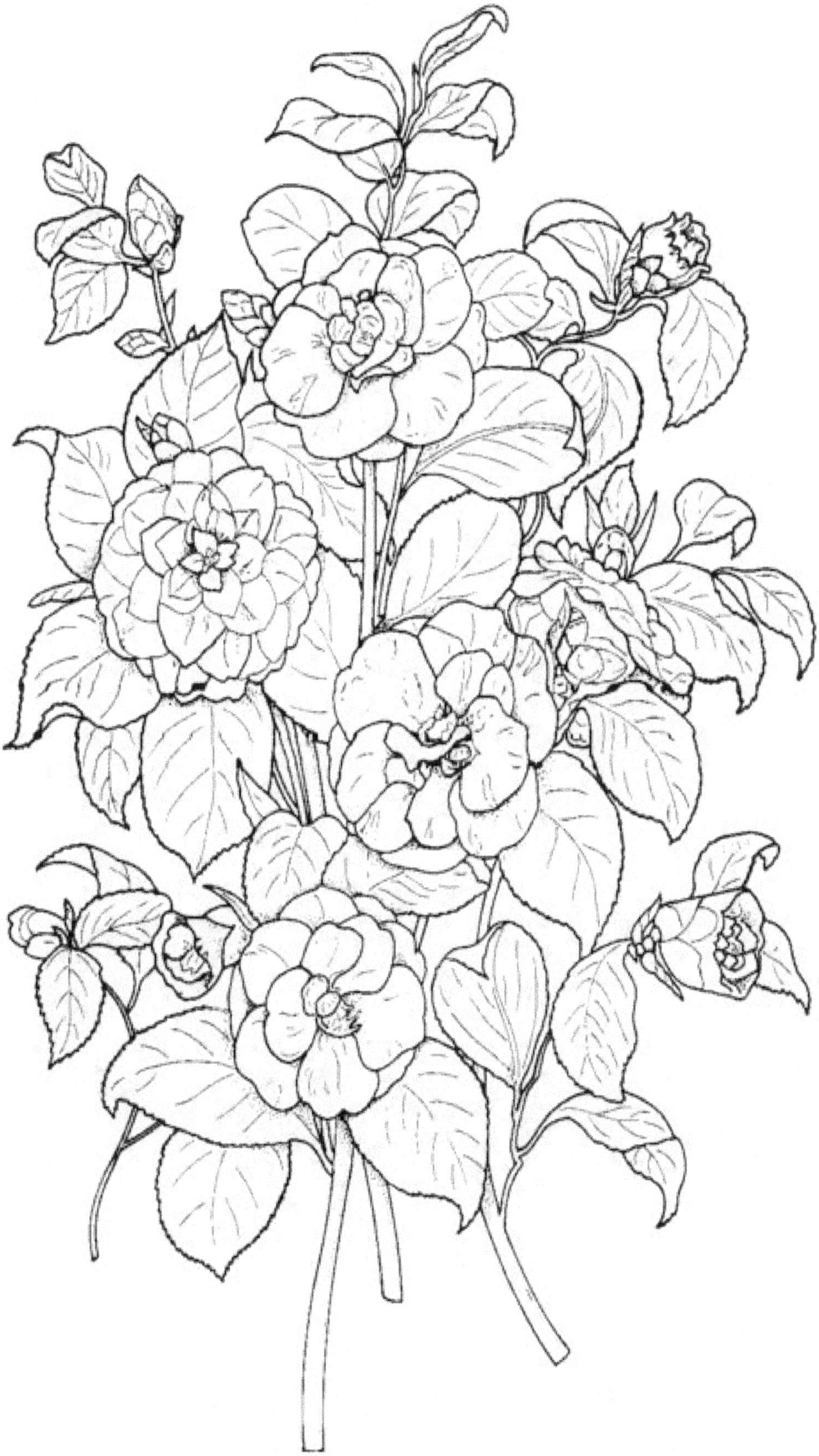

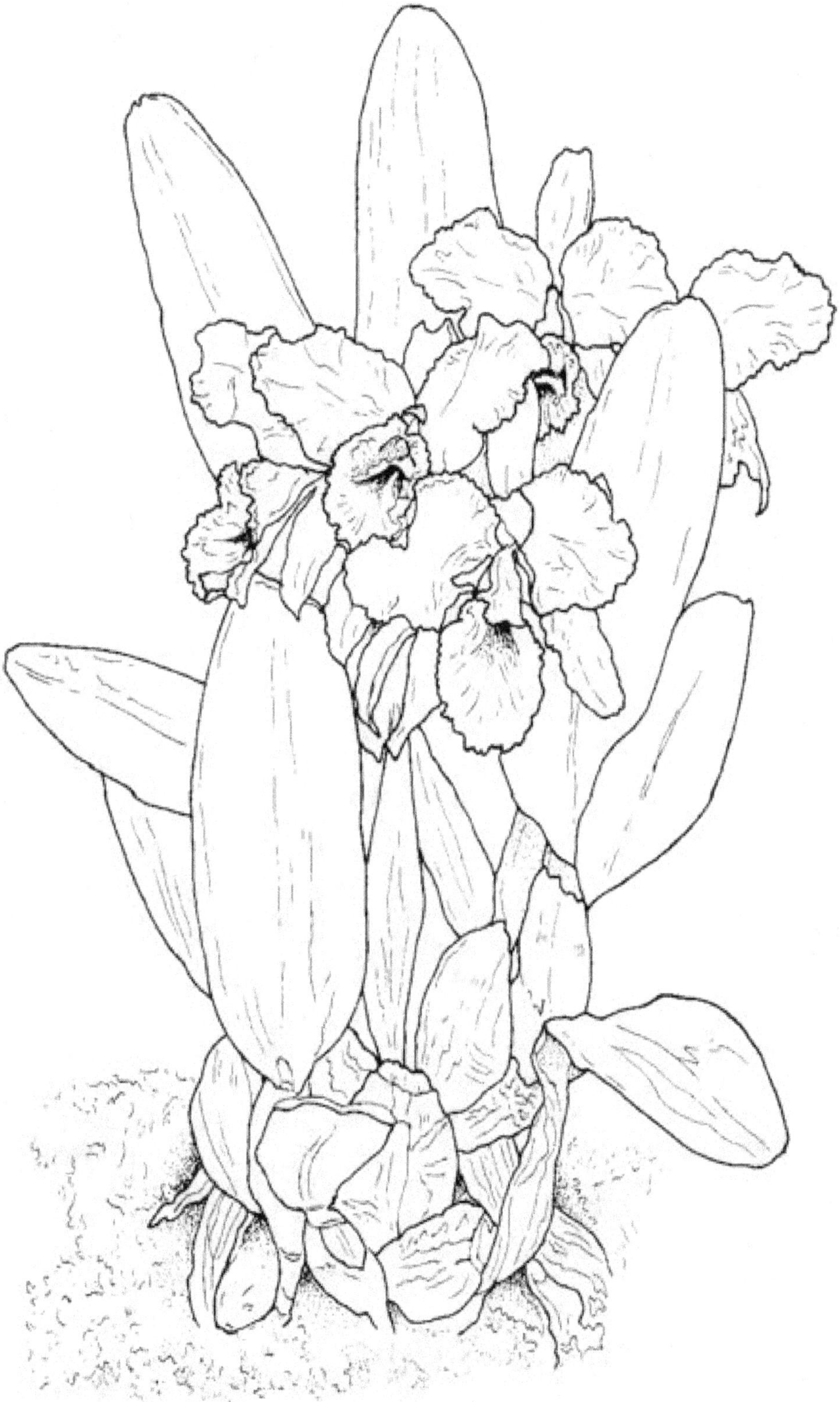

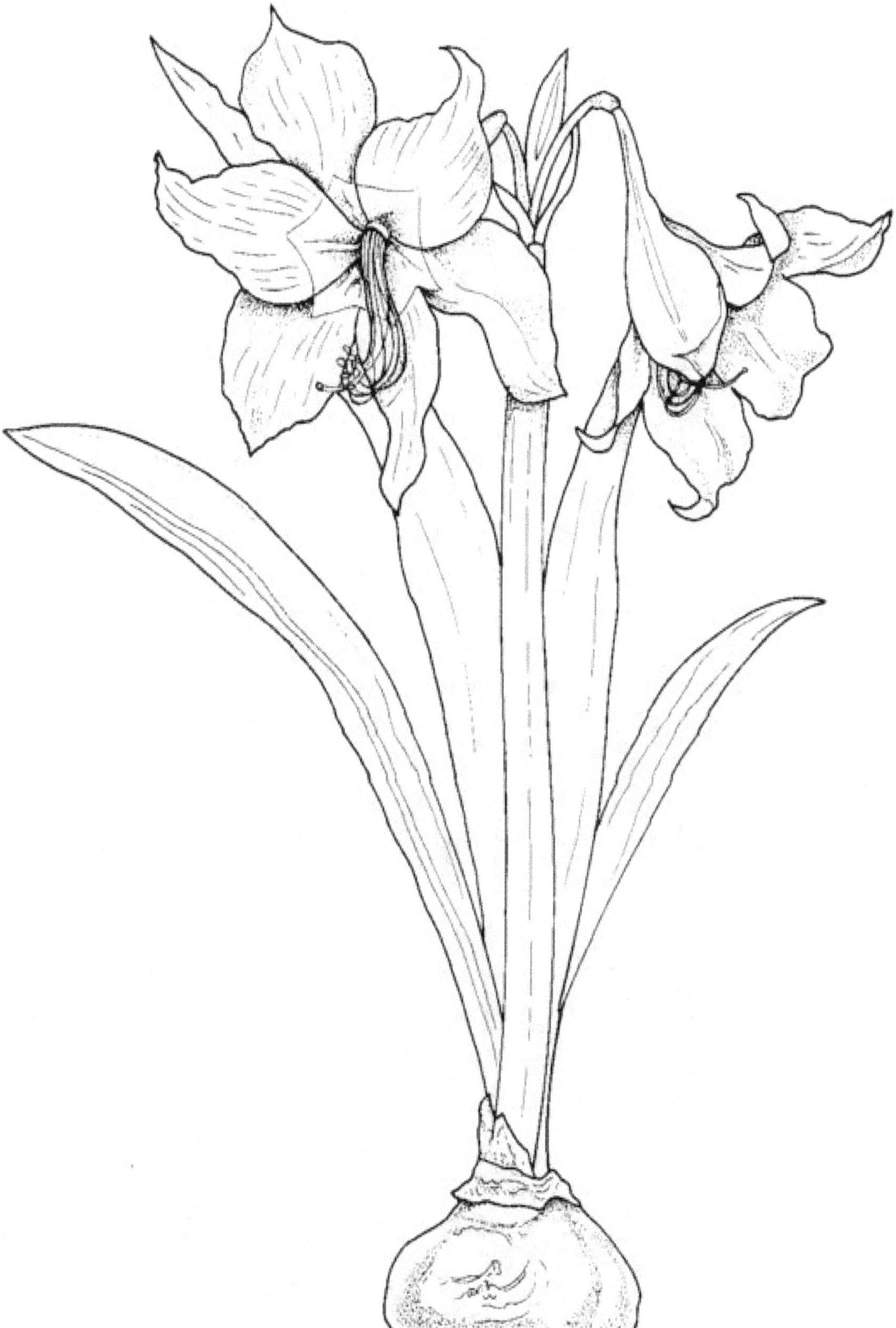

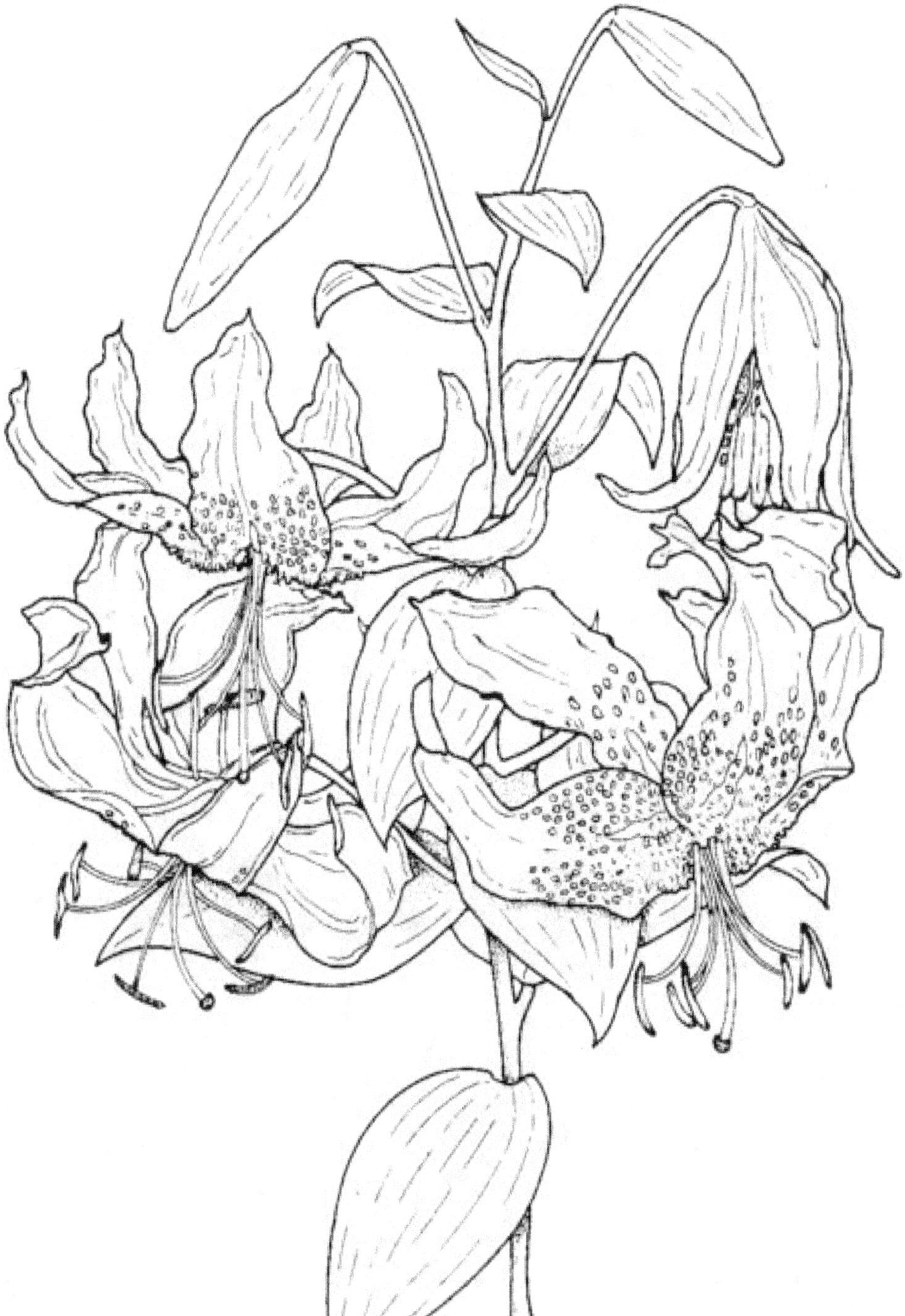

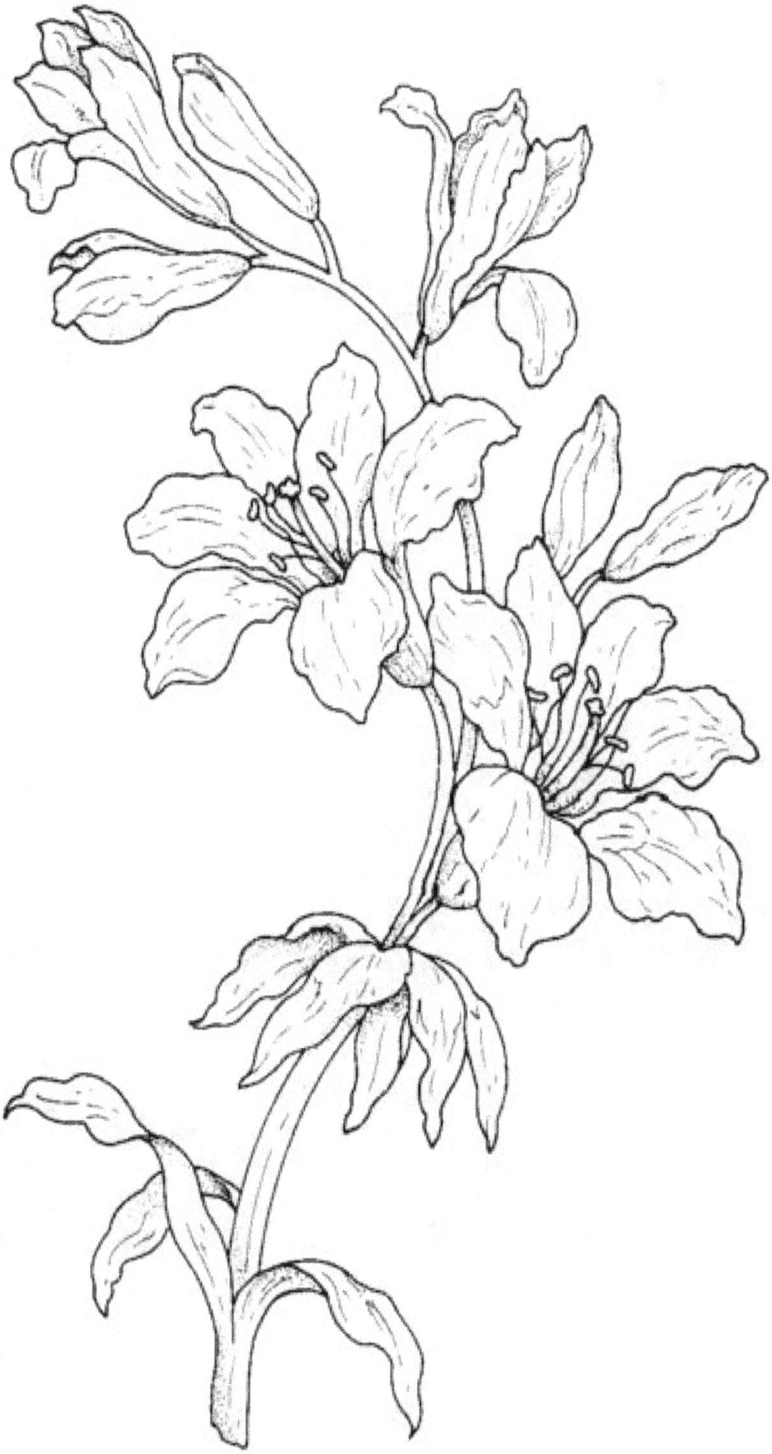

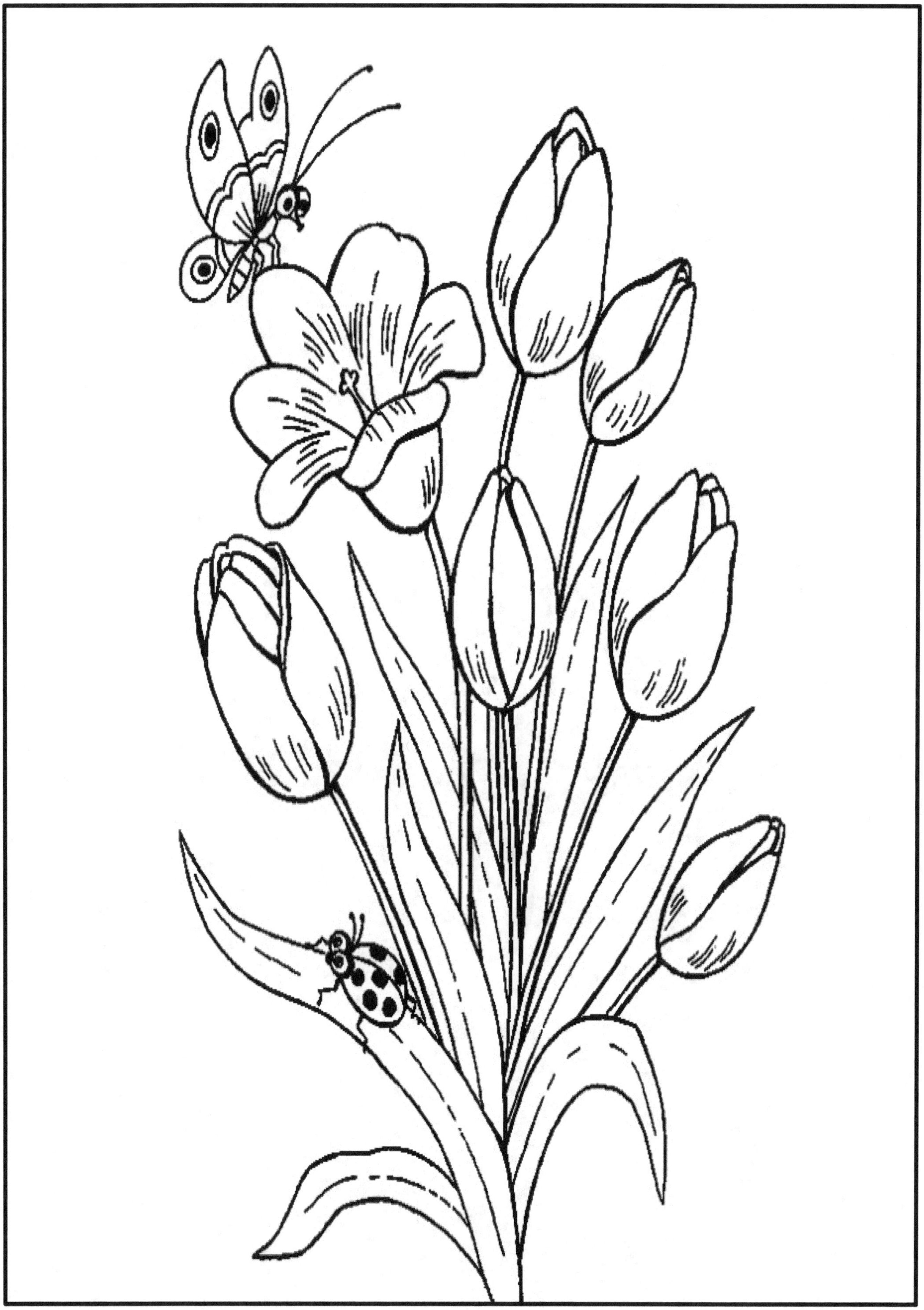

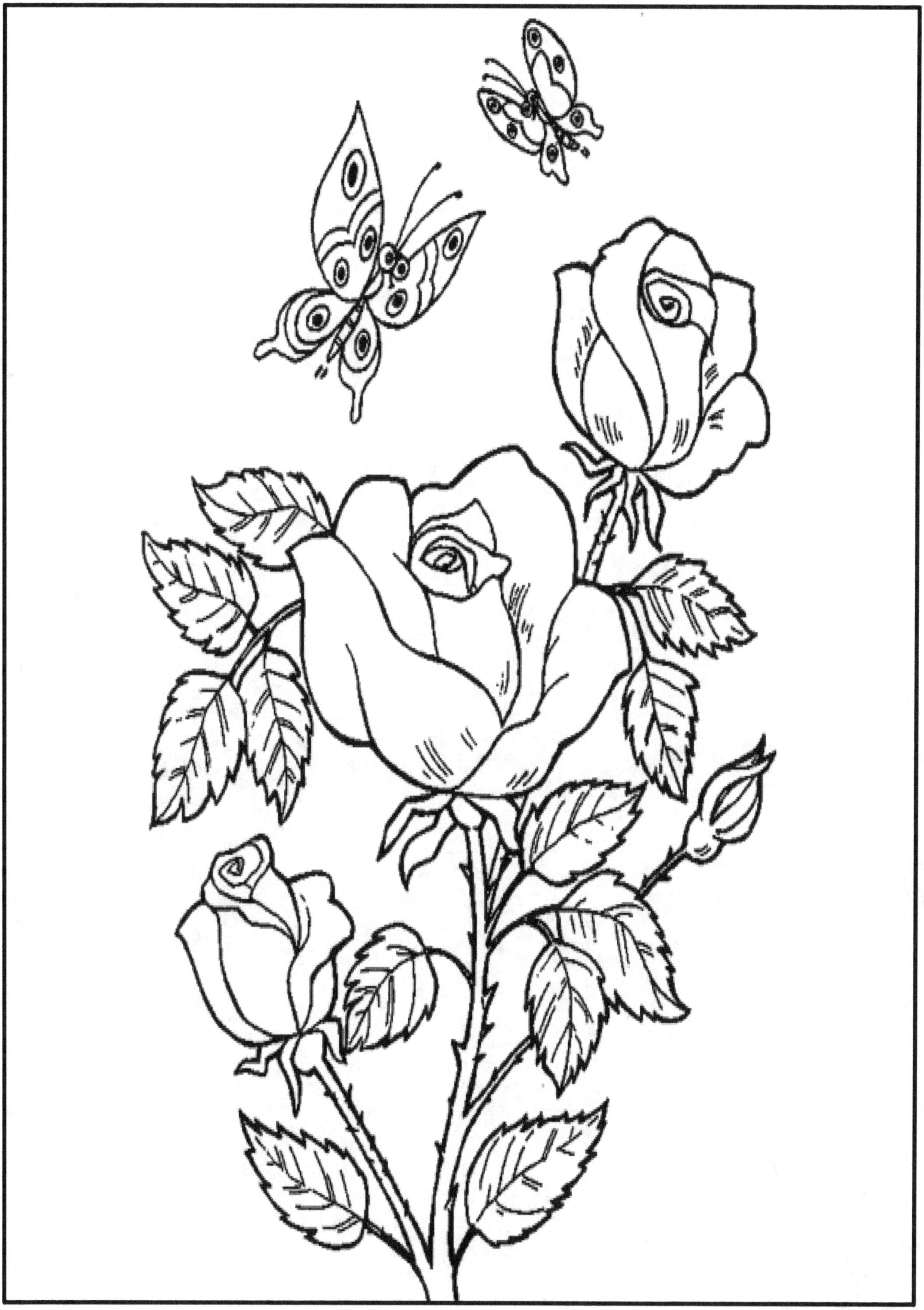

www.ingramcontent.com/pod-product-compliance
Lightning Source LLC
Chambersburg PA
CBHW081449220526
45466CB00008B/2569
* 9 7 9 8 5 9 0 5 9 7 5 4 3 *